Threshold to Music

SECOND EDITION

Level Two Teacher's Resource Book

ELEANOR KIDD
MUSIC CONSULTANT
Richmond, California

Fearon Pitman Publishers, Inc.
Belmont, California

Acknowledgments

Credit and grateful appreciation are due the publishers and owners for use of the following songs. Any omissions are due to the difficulty in finding the source of the material and can be corrected by contacting Fearon Publishers, Inc., Belmont, California.

"Good bye, Old Paint," "Au Claire de la Lune," "On Top of Old Smoky," "The Hole in the Bucket," and "The Echo" from *Making Music Your Own, Books Three and Four,* Silver Burdett Company, Division of General Learning Corporation. © 1971. Used by permission.

"Old Woman," "Chairs to Mend," and "This Train" from *Books Three, Four, and Five* of *Exploring Music* by Eunice Boardman, and Beth Landis, Holt, Rinehart and Winston, Inc. © 1971, 1966. Used by permission.

"Canoe Round" from *Chansons de Notre Chalet,* Cooperative Recreation Service, Inc. Used by permission.

"Kookaburra" by M. Sinclair from *The Ditty Bag* compiled by Jane Tobitt. Used by permission.

"Frog Music" by Gertrude Mander and Harvey W. Loomis, from *Discovering Music Together, Books Three and Four,* by Beatrice Perham Krone, Charles Leonhard, Irving Wolfe, and Margaret Fullerton. Copyright © 1966, 1970 by Follet Educational Corporation, a division of Follet Corporation. Used by permission.

"Old Texas" and "Mr. Banjo" adapted from *Singing with Children* by Nye, Nye, Aubin, and Kyme. © 1962 by Wadsworth Publishing Company, Inc., Belmont, California, 94002. Reprinted by permission of publisher.

Appreciation and thanks are also given to the teachers and pupils of the Richmond Unified School District, California, for their cooperation and whole-hearted enthusiasm in proving many of the concepts presented in this book. Thanks, also, to Julie Kranhold for her never-ending patience.

Cover Art: "Dog Barking at the Moon" by Joan Miro (Oil on Canvas, 1926). Reproduced by permission of the Philadelphia Museum of Art; the A. E. Gallatin Collection; Photo by Alfred J. Wyatt.
Edited and Designed by Julie Kranhold
Illustrated by Darcy Paige
Photographs by John Monroe

ISBN 0-8224-9064-1

Printed in the United States of America

Foreword

Recent years have generated new insights concerning purposes and methods of music education. One of the major thrusts has been toward the totality of music education with special attention to music as it is heard, felt, imagined, and created. The aural nature of music is being placed once again in the center of the music experience. The development of aural acuity becomes the basis for improved performance, improvisation, and creative activities.

The *Threshold to Music, Second Edition,* exemplifies this contemporary emphasis in teaching music to children. Rhythmic comprehension, melodic contour, feeling for phrasing, and dynamics and pitch contrast are all approached through the ear and body movement.

Visual matters are presented only after aural recognition and body response have provided a foundation for musical learning. Inner hearing, seeing what one hears, and hearing what one sees are integral features of the lessons presented.

The program proceeds in sequential fashion, and lessons are carefully outlined in a way that makes them very attractive to classroom teachers who need such support to build confidence in teaching their own music. One of the outstanding features is the use of charts instead of books, making it possible for the teacher to pinpoint class attention on the concepts presented. Without concentrated eye involvement with the score as music is heard, studied, and sung, music reading ability will not develop. Thus, the use of such charts helps to overcome one of the weaknesses of much music teaching, and raises the level of music literacy.

KARL D. ERNST
Past President International Society for Music Education
Past President Music Educators National Conference
Past Professor Music Education, California State University, Hayward

Contents

Musical Terms

Accent The stress of one tone over others, usually on the first beat.

Alla breve A tempo mark (¢) indicating duple time with the half note (♩) rather than the quarter note as the beat.

Anacrusis Upbeat or pickup which indicates a melody begins with an incomplete measure.

Bar lines Lines dividing a certain number of beats into measures.

Beat The basic unit of time in music, usually organized in groups of two or three.

Cadence A musical resting place at the end of a phrase or section of a composition.

Canon A composition in which all parts have the same melody but start at different points.

Chord A simultaneous sounding of three or more tones.

Crescendo A gradual increase in volume of sound indicated by the sign <.

Decrescendo A gradual decrease in volume of sound indicated by the sign >.

Diatonic The order of notes as found on the white keys of the piano, using whole steps and half-steps.

Dotted notes A dot placed after a note adds to it one-half of its value.

Double bar Two vertical lines drawn through the staff to indicate the end of the section or composition.

Down beat The downward motion given by the conductor to indicate the beginning beat of a measure.

Duple meter The regular grouping of time units in two.

Dynamics Varying and contrasting degrees of intensity or loudness.

Echo clapping Clapping a given rhythm pattern but starting after one or more measures (patterns) have been clapped.

Eighth note A unit of musical notation (♪) that receives one-half the time value of the quarter note.

Eighth rest A symbol (ɣ) used to indicate a period of silence equal to one eighth note.

Flat The symbol (♭) which indicates the lowering of the pitch of a note by one half-step.

Form The organization of all elements of a composition to achieve aesthetic logic.

Forte Italian word meaning loud and strong, abbreviated to *f*.

Fortissimo Very loud, abbreviated to *ff*.

Half-note The half-note receives half the value of a whole note and receives two pulses when the lower number of the time signature is four (♩).

Half-rest The sign (▬) indicating silence corresponding to the half-note.

Hand singing The use of hand signals for each note of a melody. Illustrations can be found in the Appendix, on page 88.

Improvise To create a rhythm or melody spontaneously.

Inner hearing Hearing the melodic pattern within the body without singing or playing.

Ledger lines Short lines drawn through the stems of notes which are too high or low to be represented on the staff.

Major A mode derived from the major scale and distinguished by the use of the major third (C to E) and with a half-step between the third-fourth and seventh-eighth steps of the scale.

Measure The space between two bar lines.

Melodic contour A melody pictured by a line drawing or other notation.

Meter The basic scheme of note values and accents which remain unaltered throughout the composition.

Minor A mode derived from the minor scale and distinguished by the use of the minor third (C to E♭). The sixth and seventh degrees of the scale may vary, both ascending and descending.

Mystery song Recognition of a familiar song by rhythm pattern or hand signals.

Octave An interval consisting of eight diatonic notes.

Ostinato Italian, meaning stubborn. A clearly defined musical figure which is persistently repeated, usually by the same voice or pitch.

Pattern A succession of notes which forms a recognizable unit.

Pentatonic A scale of five tones with no half-steps between any two tones. Related to the five black keys on the piano.

Phrase A natural division of the melodic line, comparable to a sentence in speech.

Piano Italian for soft. Indicated by p.

Pianissimo Very soft, indicated by pp.

Quarter note A unit of notation that receives one pulse when the lower number of the time signature is four (♩).

Quarter rest A sign (𝄽) indicating silence corresponding to the value of a quarter note.

Repeat signs A sign signifying that the music between ‖: and :‖ is to be repeated.

Rhythm Notes of different duration combined in sequence to create a pattern.

Rondo A composition characterized by the principle theme being repeated after each new theme is introduced.

Sixteenth note A unit of musical notation that receives one-half the time value of an eighth note (♪).

Sixteenth rest A symbol (𝄾) used to indicate a period of silence equal to one sixteenth note.

Sharp The symbol (♯) which indicates the raising of a note by one half-step.

Syncopation The deliberate upsetting of the normal pulse of meter, accent, and rhythm.

Tempo Italian for time, with regard to speed. Pace at which a composition is to be performed.

Tetrachord A succession of four tones which is the basis for constructing a scale.

Tie A curved line placed over a note and its repetition to show that the two should be performed as one unbroken note.

Triad A chord of three tones.

Triplet A group of three notes performed in place of two notes of the same value indicated by a three and a bracket ($\frac{3}{\sqcap}$).

Whole note The largest single unit of modern music notation receiving a value of four pulsations in meter (𝅝).

Whole rest A pause or silence equal in length to a whole note (▬).

Introduction

   The second edition of the *Threshold to Music* is greatly influenced by the pedagogy of Zoltán Kodály. In keeping with Professor Kodály's belief that all children should be provided with musical skills, this program will enable the teacher to present a developmental approach to the reading and writing of music.
   To the teacher:
   - who feels that the teaching of music is not one of his or her strengths, either through lack of experience or training, and, therefore, lack of interest,
   - who has little or no help from a music specialist due to scheduling or financial needs of the school district,
   - who feels there can be musical experiences other than the conventional "songbook-record" approach,

the *Threshold to Music* will provide a stepping stone to rewarding musical experiences involving singing, music reading, and participation.

   The teacher of the self-contained classroom can have the greatest influence on a child's attitude to all learning. The teacher's enthusiasm, sense of humor, intelligence, and training can give the child experiences that cannot be duplicated. It is natural to teach from personal strengths, whether reading, language arts, science, art, physical education, or music. This is the natural desire in all of us—to be successful. Many times this desire leads to imbalance within the educational framework. Therefore, it would be ideal to have a "specialist" come into the classroom and "take over" those subject areas that are not one of the teacher's "strengths," but until that ideal becomes a reality, the classroom teacher must try to be all-knowing in the various programs offered in the schools.

For ease of planning, the *Teacher's Resource Book* contains a miniature of each class-room chart with each lesson. Although it might be a temptation to present the classroom charts at the beginning of each lesson, greater success will be achieved by the utilization of preparatory experiences. Rhythmic and melodic activities should be presented at the beginning of the school year, using familiar songs from previous experiences.

BASIC RHYTHMIC AND MELODIC ACTIVITIES

- Sing many songs—folk songs, nursery rhymes, camp songs, and spirituals.
- Start the day with a song, take a break with a song, create new words to a familiar song.
- Call the daily roll using sol–mi (G to E on the piano); the children will echo their name. For example,

	Teacher sings	Mary echoes
	Ma–ry	I'm here
	(sol) (mi)	(sol) (mi)

- Use rhythmic activities at various times of the day, to relieve tensions, to provide a transition from one subject to another, to teach children to listen and follow directions, and to give children an opportunity for leadership. For example,

Sing a song and *clap* the **beat.**

Sing a song and *step* the **beat.**

Sing a song, *walk* the **beat,** *change direction* at the end of the **phrase.**

Sing a song and *clap* the **pattern** (syllables of the words).

• Build a musical vocabulary through a song to provide the children with experiences that will lead to success when presented with the classroom charts. See the list of "Musical Terms" presented in this book on page 7.

The *Preparation for the Chart* in the *Teacher's Resource Book* may be presented several days prior to introducing the charts to the class.

It will be obvious to those who read the material that each lesson presents more activities than can be accomplished successfully in a single music lesson. The *Other Songs to Use* and *Additional Activities* provide the teacher with a variety of enrichment experiences that will fit the needs and individuality of the children in the classroom.

The second edition of the *Threshold to Music* will enable the classroom teacher to discover the excitement of learning how to learn through music. The involvement of the teacher and child in rhythm and song through the use of the classroom charts will provide musical perception and awareness that can be related to all learning. To understand the potential this program can offer, one need only remember the old Chinese proverb: "He who hears, forgets; he who sees, remembers; but he who does, knows."

E.K.

1
Dr. Foster

Dr. Foster

do
Doc - tor Fos - ter went to Glouces-ter

3

mi
In a show-er of rain.

Dr. Foster
continued

3

sol
Stepped in a pud - dle,
Up to his mid - dle,

3

do
Nev - er went there a - gain.

Note: The children will read the song directly from the chart, so the song is not included here.

PREPARATION FOR THE CHART

1. Review previous rhythmic activities:
   - **Echo clapping**
   - Clapping a **pattern** and stepping the **beat.**
   - Stepping a pattern and clapping the beat.
   - Singing **mystery songs** from Level 1.
   - Singing familiar songs and turning the **phrase.**
   - Using flash cards with rhythm patterns and tone-syllable patterns.

2. Review previous melodic activities:
   - Echo singing with hand signals and tone syllables.
   - Using hand signals for a familiar song without singing (mystery song).

INTRODUCE THE CHART

1. Establish the beat by saying "one, two, ready, clap." (Move from Chart 1 to Chart 2 without losing the beat.)
2. Read and clap the two charts with rhythm syllables. Be sure to observe the **repeat signs.**
3. Read the words and clap the pattern:

Note: "Gloucester" is pronounced "Glau-ster."

4. Read the words and step the pattern.
5. Read the words, step the pattern, and clap the beat.
6. Choose one child to keep the beat on the chart while the class reads and claps the pattern and steps the beat.
7. Establish the pitch for "do." Sing both charts with tone syllables and arm signals.

Note: Check the rhythmic pattern of the triplet; the tendency is to rush the tempo.

8. Establish the pitch for "do."
   - Choose one child to sing the first line using the arm signal.
   - Choose another child to sing the sec-

ond line with the tone syllable for mi, using arm signals.
- Continue this activity through the second chart.

9. Sing both charts and dramatize the position of the intervals:
   - do—fists on the floor
   - mi—slap the knees
   - sol—stand up and clap
   - do'—stand up with fists overhead

10. Repeat the last activity, using **dynamics:**
    - Begin the song softly (p, **piano**).
    - Gradually get louder ($<$, **crescendo**).
    - End the song loudly (f, **forte**). Do not allow the children to shout.
    - You may wish to write the dynamic markings on the chart.

11. Divide the class and sing the song as a round, using hand signals.

Note: The number of groups depends on the musical ability of your class. The song can be sung in two, three, or four parts.

OTHER SONGS TO USE

Let the children make rhythm charts of other familiar rounds for the class to use: "Are You Sleeping?" • "Scotland's Burning" • "French Cathedrals."

ADDITIONAL ACTIVITIES

1. Divide the class into four groups, and step the rhythm pattern as a round.
2. Choose four children to each sing one line of the song, while using hand signals.
3. Choose four children to sing the song as a round, using hand signals. The success

of this activity will depend on the musical ability and maturity of your class.

4. Have four children select different rhythm instruments and each play one line of the chart. Each child must enter without losing the beat. For example,
   - sticks: ⊓ ⊓ ⊓ ⊓
   - wood block: ⊓ ⊓³ | ⌡ ♩
   - tambourine: ⊓³ ⊓ ⊓³ ⊓
   - drum: ⊓³ ⊓ | ⌡ ♩

5. Use the last activity and play as a four part round.
6. Distribute the C–E–G–C' resonator bells to four children.
   - Ask the children to discover which tone syllable their bell sounds.
   - Play the song on the bells, either one line at a time or as a four part round.

7. Choose four children to play the bells as a **chord** (three or more tones played simultaneously). Play the chord on the beat while the class sings the song, either in unison or as a round.
8. Select one line of the chart to play or sing as an **ostinato.**

Note: The more musically advanced class will enjoy creating their own ostinato.

EVALUATION OF RHYTHMIC AND PERCEPTUAL SKILLS

Psychomotor Development and Perception

1. Can the children demonstrate motor control while clapping or stepping a rhythm pattern?
   - Moving from three (⊓³) to two (⊓) to one (I), without losing the beat

2. Can they dramatize the positions of the intervals?
   - Moving from low "do" to mi, then sol, and high "do"

Aural and Visual Acuity and Perception

1. Can the children discover the major third (do–mi) when "do" is established?
2. Can they discover the minor third (mi–sol) when the mi is established?
3. Can they discover the perfect fourth (sol–do') when the sol is established?
4. Can they differentiate the triplet (⊓³) and the eighth notes (⊓), dividing each beat into three and two equal parts?
5. Can they read and interpret the rhythm symbols on the chart correctly?

Can You Read?

Clap a Canon

Note: Because the next two charts teach the same basic concept, the "Evaluation of Rhythmic and Perceptual Skills" appears at the end of Lesson 3.

PREPARATION FOR THE CHART

1. Prepare the children for more difficult rhythm patterns by extending the length of the pattern and incorporating various rhythmic activities. For example,
   - Echo clapping with a student leader using eight beats (two **measures**).
   - Varying the sound of each pattern: clapping, tapping, rapping, stepping, etc.
   - **Inner hearing**–mystery song: Clap the pattern of the first phrase of a familiar song. When the song has been identified, use inner hearing with flash cards. Begin by singing the song, then follow directions on the flash cards but do not sing.

| sing | step | tap | clap |

INTRODUCE THE CHART

1. Read and clap the entire chart with rhythm syllables, keeping the beat on the chart as you move from line to line. Establish the beat by saying "One, two, ready, clap." Be sure to observe the repeat signs.
2. When you feel the children are secure with the rhythm pattern, clap a **canon:**
   - Teacher claps the first phrase (| | ⊓ |).
   - Class begins clapping the chart when the teacher begins the second phrase.
   Write the canon on the chalkboard:

Teacher ‖: | | ⊓ | ‖: ⊓³ ⊓³ | | | ⊓ ⊓ ⊓| | ↋ | ↋ :‖

Class ‖: | | ⊓ | ⊓³ ⊓³ | | | ⊓ ⊓ ⊓| :‖ | ↋ | ↋ :‖

3. Select two children to read and clap the chart as a canon.

OTHER SONGS TO USE

1. Clap the chart while singing a familiar song. "Yankee Doodle" • "Four in a Boat" • "Camptown Races."
2. Sing the song, step the beat, and clap the chart.

ADDITIONAL ACTIVITIES

1. Clap the chart, one line at a time, for **dictation.** For example,

Teacher claps	Class echoes and writes
I I ⊓ I	I I ⊓ I
	ta ta ti-ti ta
⊓̅³ I ⅃ I	⌢³ I ⅃ I
	triple-ti, ta, rest, ta

2. If the children are confident with tone syllables and intervals, let them write the tone syllables under the pattern they have written. Give each child an opportunity to sing his melody.

Note: Have the shy or insecure child write his melody on the chalkboard for the class to sing.

3. Encourage the children to write words to the melodic pattern they have written. For example,

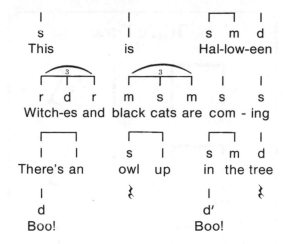

s	l	s m	d
This	is	Hal-low-een	
r d r	m s m	s	s
Witch-es and	black cats are	com	- ing
I I	s l	s m	d
There's an	owl up	in the tree	
d	ʔ	d'	ʔ
Boo!		Boo!	

Note: Not all the children in your class will be able to perform this activity successfully. Encourage those children who are musically capable to put their original songs on a chart for the class to sing. This will encourage the children who are having difficulty.

Check the songs for syllabication and musicality before putting them on a chart. Have each child sing his song to you in case any intervals need to be altered.

4. Divide the class into four groups and read the chart with rhythm instruments. Each group plays one line of the chart:
    Group 1—sticks
    Group 2—wood block
    Group 3—tambourine
    Group 4—triangle

5. Read and play the chart as a canon. Tell the children how many times they are to repeat the chart.

6. Turn to the next lesson.

Triple and Duple Time

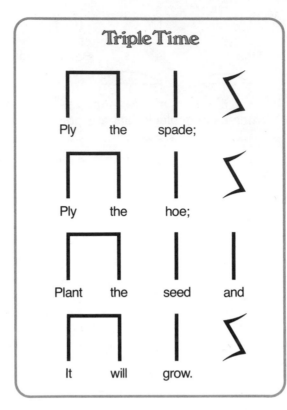

Triple Time

Ply the spade;

Ply the hoe;

Plant the seed and

It will grow.

Duple Time

Thog - gle snog - gle

Clum - ber Thud.

Thun - der - dud Drin - kum

Thim - ble - bug.

PREPARATION FOR THE CHARTS

Note: Charts 3a and 3b present rhythmic experiences in triple and duple time. The children were introduced to triple time in the Level 1 charts. The time signature for 3/4 will be presented on succeeding charts and lessons as ³.

INTRODUCE CHART 3a

1. Read the words of the chart with the class. Keep the beat as you move from line to line.
2. Read and clap the chart with rhythm syllables.
3. Read the chart with the words and clap the beat. How many beats do they feel? (3)

4. Clap the beat and step the pattern while speaking the words.
5. Step the beat and act out the words:

Ply the spade (push the spade, throw dirt on the "rest")

Ply the hoe (hoe the ground, wipe brow on the "rest")

Plant the seed and (put seed in the ground, and pat the dirt)

It will grow (stand and jump up on "grow")

6. Read the words on the chart. Clap the pattern and step the beat. Accent the first beat by stepping hard and bending the knees. Tiptoe on the second and third beats:

Ply the spade
stamp tip – toe

7. Choose a leader to clap the chart, line by line. Have the class echo the pattern and write the rhythm symbols.
8. Have the children put tone syllables under the patterns they wrote in the last activity. Ask several children to sing their melodies.

Note: Some children will be able to establish their beginning pitch, others may need assistance.

INTRODUCE CHART 3b

1. Read the words with the class. Point to the beats as they read the chart.
2. Read and clap the chart with rhythm syllables and step the beat. How many beats do they feel? (2)
3. Continue this chart, using the same activities as introduced in Chart 3a.

ADDITIONAL ACTIVITIES

1. Go back to Chart 1.
   - Establish the beat (fairly slow).
   - Clap the beat and say the rhythm syllables. Move from chart to chart, without losing the beat.

2. Begin on Chart 1 again.
   - Step the beat.
   - Clap the pattern with rhythm syllables.
   - Accent the first beat by stepping hard and bending the knees. (Keep the beat steady as you move from duple to triple meter.)

3. Begin on Chart 1.
   - Establish the beat.
   - Step the beat, clap and say the rhythm syllables.
   - At a given signal (rap the desk or ring a bell), read the chart silently but continue to step the beat (inner hearing).
   - Repeat the signal and continue clapping and rhythm syllables. (Did the children all begin on the same place on the chart? Repeat this activity several times in order to insure success.)

4. Repeat the above activity but just read the rhythm syllables. Do not clap the pattern or step the beat. This exercise will help to promote silent reading.

5. Using Chart 3b, create original words to the rhythm pattern based on classroom subject areas:

Social Studies

Kan-sas,   U-tah,

Il-li   -   nois,

O-re-gon, Tex-as,

Del-a   -   ware.

Health or Foods

lem-on,   peach-es,

a-pri   -   cots,

straw-ber-ries, ap-ples,

nec-tar   -   ines.

Note: Let the children decide which subject area to use and create their own word patterns to fit the rhythm pattern.

6. Use tone syllables with Chart 3b and create an original song. Let some of the children sing their original melodies to the class.

Note: In case any changes need to be made, be sure to go over the melody with each child individually before he presents his song to the class. This will avoid any embarrassment.

EVALUATION OF RHYTHMIC AND PERCEPTUAL SKILLS

Psychomotor Development and Perception

1. Are the children becoming more confident while performing extended and diverse rhythms such as clapping or stepping duple and triple meters?
2. Are they becoming more aware of the accent and beat while performing rhythmic motor activities?

Aural and Visual Acuity and Perception

1. Can the children hear and feel the basic rhythms (duple and triple) while they clap a pattern?
2. Can they hear and identify the rhythm patterns of words?
3. Can they hear familiar intervals (Level 1) and apply them to a rhythm pattern?
4. Can they read rhythm patterns in duple or triple meter?

Musical Development and Social Maturity

1. Can the children create their own melodic phrases to a given rhythmic pattern?
2. Are more children volunteering to perform their original melodies for the class?

The Tie

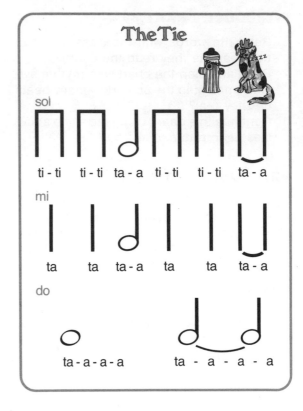

The Tie

PREPARATION FOR THE CHART

Note: The children were introduced to the half-note (♩) in Chart 38 of Level 1.

Tell the children the curved line on the chart is called a **tie.** The tie connects two notes of the same pitch. The tones are connected and played or sung for the combined duration.

INTRODUCE THE CHART

1. Read the first line of the chart with clapping and rhythm syllables.
2. Ask one child to read the second line of the chart with clapping and rhythm syllables. Have the class echo if he is correct.

3. Read and clap the third line of the chart with the class.
4. Ask one child to be the leader and read and clap the entire chart.
5. To reinforce the concept of note values, use a piece of paper. Tell the children that it represents a whole note. Fold the paper in half:

How many halves are there? (2) Unfold the paper. How many half-notes will equal a whole note? Now fold the paper in fourths:

Before unfolding the paper, ask the class, how many fourths equal one half? (2) How many fourths equal one whole? (4) Unfold the paper to show the relationship. Fold the paper into eighths and continue to demonstrate the relationship to musical notes:

Note: The more mature children will immediately relate this to mathematics and will want to continue using the sequence.

Relate mathematical values to musical note values on the chalkboard:

$1 = \circ$
$\frac{1}{2} = \downarrow \qquad \downarrow$
$\frac{1}{4} = \mid \quad \mid \quad \mid \quad \mid$
$\frac{1}{8} = \sqcap \; \sqcap \; \sqcap \; \sqcap$

For those who wish to continue the sequence:

$\frac{1}{16}$ =

$\frac{1}{32}$ =

$\frac{1}{64}$ =

trill

Note: This concept can be fascinating to some children and should be developed within the musical capabilities of the teacher and children.

6. Establish the pitch for sol. Sing the first line of the chart with hand signals, giving the half-note and the tied notes their full value by stepping the beat.
7. Continue with lines two and three. Step the beat, and sing with tone syllables and hand signals.
8. Divide the class into three groups. Establish the pitch for sol, and have all groups step the beat. In addition,
    Group 1 sings the first line
    Group 2 sings the second line
    Group 3 sings the third line
9. Divide the class into three groups and sing the chart as a round; repeat the chart three times.
10. After the children are confident singing the chart as a round, give a signal (clap or ring bell) for them to hold the tone

they are singing until you give another signal for them to continue the chart.
- Stepping the beat will give the children confidence.
- Ask the children what they heard when they held the tone. (The **chord** or **triad** was introduced in Chart 35 of Level 1.)

OTHER SONGS TO USE

Clap the pattern on the chart, step the beat, and sing a familiar song: "Yankee Doodle" • "Are You Sleeping?" • "Marching to Praetoria." (You will probably have to repeat the chart several times to complete the song.)

ADDITIONAL ACTIVITIES

1. Choose appropriate instruments to read the chart and play as an accompaniment to a familiar song. For example,
    - "Are You Sleeping?"—triangle
    - "Yankee Doodle"—drum
    - "Marching to Praetoria"—sticks or wood block
2. Create words to the pattern on the chart.

   ⊓   ⊓   ♩   ⊓   ⊓   ♩
   I am ve - ry tired, I am ve - ry tired.

   | | ♩ | | ♩
   Go   to   bed, Go   to   bed.

   ∘   ∘
   Sleep – –,   Sleep – –.

   - Be sure to hold each note for its full value.
   - Put tone syllables to the pattern and sing as a round, repeating several times.
3. Make flash cards, and give each child an opportunity to clap one of the patterns:

EVALUATION OF RHYTHMIC AND PERCEPTUAL SKILLS

Psychomotor Development and Perception

Can the children step or clap various rhythm patterns using whole ($\circ$), half ($\downarrow$), or tied notes ($\mid\underline{\;}\mid$, $\downarrow\underline{\;}\downarrow$)?

Aural and Visual Acuity and Perception

1. Can the children hear and differentiate the value of the notes presented so far?

2. Can they sing a given tone and maintain the pitch while other tones are being sung (chord)?
3. Can they read the symbols for whole and half-notes?

Mystery Songs

1.
l s l d l s m r d

2.
m m r m d d s s m s r r

3.
d d d r m r d m r r d

PREPARATION FOR THE CHART

Goodbye, Old Paint

Note: This is a review song from Level 1, Chart 46.

1. Clap the rhythm pattern as a mystery song. If the children have forgotten the melody, you may have to reteach the song. (Other verses may be found in folk-song books or music texts.)
2. Sing the song, swaying back and forth to the pulse (one sway to each measure):

sway   sway   sway   sway

3. Sing the song, sway the pulse, and step the beat.
   - How many steps did the children take to each sway? (3)
   - Does the song start on the first beat? (no)
   - What is the name of the beat before the first beat in the measure? (**anacrusis,** Level 1, Chart 8.)

My Lord, What a Morning

1. Teach the song.

   *Note: This song provides an introduction to **syncopation,** which will be developed further on later charts. The accent does not occur on the first beat of the measure.*

2. Teach all three verses.
   - Encourage the children to use musical discrimination. Which verse should be sung softly (p)? (the second verse)
   - Give individual children the opportunity to sing one verse as a solo. Have the class sing the chorus.

GOODBYE, OLD PAINT

Cowboy Song

Refrain   Fine

Good - bye,   Old   Paint,   I'm 'leav - in' Chey - enne.

D.C.

My foot's   in   the   stir - rup,   my   pon - y   won't stand,
I'm leav - in' Chey - enne . . .   I'm   off   for   Mon - tan'

MY LORD, WHAT A MORNING

Spiritual

My Lord, what a morn - ing,

My Lord, what a morn - ing,

My Lord, what a morn - ing,

Fine

When the stars be - gin to fall.

1. You'll hear the trum - pet sound.
2. You'll hear the sin - ners mourn.
3. You'll hear the Chris - tians shout.

To wake the na - tions un - der-ground.
To wake the na - tions un - der-ground.
To wake the na - tions un - der-ground.

Look - ing to my God's right hand,

D.C. al fine

When the stars be - gin to fall.

AU CLAIR DE LA LUNE

Traditional French Song

Au clair de la lu - ne, Mon a - mi Pier - rot,

Pre - te - moi ta plu - me, Pour e - crire un mot;

Ma chan-delle est mor - te, Je n'ai plus de feu;

Ou - vre moi ta por - te, Pour l'a-mour de Dieu.

Phonetic Pronunciation:

Oh klehr duh lah loo-nuh,
    mohn ah-mee pee-ehr-oh,
Preh-tuh mwah tah ploo-muh,
    poor ay-dreer uhn moh;
Mah shahn-dehl eh mohr-tuh,
    zhuh nay ploo duh fooh;
Oov-ruh mwah tah pohr-tuh,
    poor lah moor duh dee-ooh.

English Translation:

In the silvery moonlight,
    My dear friend, Pierrot,
Please lend me your pen, sir,
    I will write a note;
My candle is dying,
    Matches I have not;
Open up your door, sir,
    For the love of God.

Au Clair de la Lune

1. Teach the song. The children will enjoy singing the song in French.
2. Sing the song and step the beat. Be sure to give the half-notes (♩) and whole notes (𝅝) their full value.
3. Sing the song, clap the beat, and step the pattern.
4. Sing the song, step the beat, clap the pattern, and turn the phrase.
5. How many times is the first phrase repeated? (3)
   - Sing the first phrase. Tell the children this will be shown as A or ● on the chalkboard.
   - Sing the second phrase and ask one child to show how this phrase will be shown on the chalkboard.
   - Continue through the entire song, making the phrases:

   A A B A or ● ● ▲ ●

6. Sing the song and ask one child to point to the phrases on the chalkboard as they occur.

INTRODUCE THE CHART

1. Clap one of the patterns on the chart and let the class identify the pattern by holding up one, two, or three fingers.
2. Choose one child to read and clap one of the patterns on the chart for the class to identify.
   - If the pattern is clapped correctly, the class will hold up one, two, or three fingers to correspond to the line. If the pattern is clapped incorrectly, they will keep their hands down.

3. Repeat this activity for all three patterns.
4. Clap one of the patterns on the chart.
   - Can the children identify the song?

- Ask the child who correctly identified the song to lead the class with tone syllables and hand signals.

5. Continue through the chart.
   - Clap the pattern
   - Identify the pattern
   - Sing the pattern with tone syllables and hand signals.
   - Identify the song.
   - Sing the song, using hand signals where possible.

6. "Goodbye, Old Paint" can be sung entirely with hand signals. Introduce the low sol (s,) by rote.

7. Make the hand signals for one of the phrases on the chart but *do not* sing. Have the class echo with tone syllables and hand singing.

Note: The children will probably need assistance with the starting pitch.

8. Repeat the last activity but ask one child to sing the phrase with tone syllables and hand signals.

ADDITIONAL ACTIVITIES

1. Use a rhythm pattern contained in one of the songs on the chart as an instrumental ostinato. Encourage musical discrimination. For example,

"Goodbye, Old Paint"

wood block:

jingle bells:

"My Lord, What a Morning"

1st verse—tambourine:

2nd verse—triangle or finger cymbals:

3rd verse—drum:

"Au Clair de la Lune"

triangle or finger cymbals:

small wood block:

2. Sing the song and step an ostinato.
3. Create a melodic ostinato to "Goodbye, Old Paint":

d l s   m l s

4. Create words to the ostinato:

d l s   m l s
rid-ing and   rop-ing and

5. Divide the class into two groups. Have Group 1 sing the song, and Group 2 sing the ostinato.

Note: These last activities will require some experimentation. Let the children decide which intervals sound the best with the song. Remember, dissonance is not always as unpleasant to children as it is to adults.

EVALUATION OF RHYTHMIC AND PERCEPTUAL SKILLS

Psychomotor Development and Perception

Can the children step a pattern using different note values and keep the beat while singing a song?

Aural and Visual Acuity and Perception

1. Are the children becoming more confident in identifying rhythm patterns of familiar songs?
2. Are they becoming increasingly confident while singing intervals that have been previously introduced?
3. Can they read the chart with tone syllables and hand signals?

6
Conductor's Beat

The Conductor's Beat

Measures mark meter.

PREPARATION FOR THE CHART

Note: Because the next two charts teach the same basic concept, the "Evaluation of Rhythmic and Perceptual Skills" appears at the end of Lesson 7.

1. Teach the song and use previous rhythmic experiences.
   • Sing the song, clap the pattern, step the beat.
   • Sing the song, clap the beat, step the pattern.
   • Sing the song, walk the beat, reverse the direction at the end of the fourth measure (goose) and the end of the song (thine).
   • Repeat the above activity but reverse the direction at the end of every second measure.

2. Divide the class into two, three, or four groups and sing the song as a round.

Note: The number of parts will depend on the maturity and musical capabilities of your class. It would be wise to start with two parts.

3. Sing the song and use inner hearing.
   • Sing the first two measures, stepping the beat.
   • Stop singing, put the melody inside, continue stepping the beat.
   • Sing the last two measures.

INTRODUCE THE CHART

1. Ask the children if they have ever watched a conductor leading an orchestra or choir, either at a concert or on television.
2. Did the children notice how the conductor used his arms?
   • Ask several children to demonstrate how a conductor uses his arms.
   • When one child demonstrates the first

WHY SHOULDN'T MY GOOSE

Traditional Round

Why should-n't my goose,

Grow as fat as thy goose,

When I paid for my goose,

Twice as much as thine?

beat correctly—coming straight down from his head to his chest—tell the class that he would make a fine conductor because he has a good **down beat.** There should be a slight bounce at the bottom of the down beat.

Note: If the conductor does not have a good down beat, the orchestra or choir would not be able to begin performing together.

3. Sing a familiar song that has a meter in two (2) and conduct the song with the class. Some songs are:
   "Yankee Doodle"
   "Jingle Bells"
   "Old Woman"

4. Choose one child to read and clap the pattern on the chart. Can the children identify the song?

5. Ask the child who correctly identified the song to conduct the class while they sing.

6. Sing the song and ask each child to conduct the beat at his desk, tapping his desk for the down beat.

7. Conduct the song on the desk and sing only the word that is tapped:

   "Why," "my," "grow," "thy," etc.

Note: Tell the children the first beat is accented. Add the word **accent** *to their musical vocabulary.*

8. Sing the song, step the beat, and clap the accent.

9. Sing the song and tap the accent on the chart.
   - Tell the children that each group on the chart is called a **measure.**
   - The lines dividing each group are called **bar lines.**

- Whenever a song is in groups of two with the first beat accented and the second beat lighter it is called **duple meter.**

10. Point to the time signature on the chart ($\frac{2}{4}$). This tells how many beats there are in one measure and what kind of note is given one beat.
    - There are two beats in a measure and a quarter note (ta) gets one beat.
    - The children might enjoy looking in their music books and identifying various time signatures.

OTHER SONGS TO USE

"Bingo" • "Billy Boy" • "Down at the Station."

ADDITIONAL ACTIVITIES

1. Sing the song as a round and create a rhythmic ostinato.
   - clap, snap: | |
   - slap knees, clap, snap, snap
      | | | |
   - As the children become more confident, create more difficult patterns and activities to be performed while they sing the song and walk the beat. For example, slap the knees with alternating right and left hands:

      R L R L | CLAP CLAP

   - Let the children create their own rhythmic ostinato.

2. Divide the class into four groups and read the chart as a rhythmic round. Use different sounds for each group:
   Group 1—clap the pattern
   Group 2—rap the pattern (knuckles on desk)

Group 3—tap the pattern (pencils on desk)
Group 4—pat the pattern (slap knees)

3. Choose four children to read the chart as an instrumental round:
   Child 1—sticks
   Child 2—tambourine
   Child 3—wood block
   Child 4—triangle

4. *Dictation.* Clap two measure patterns in duple rhythm. Have the class echo and write the patterns on individual rhythm charts.

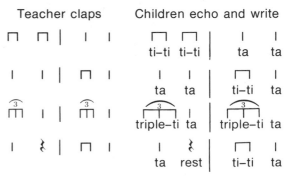

Teacher claps / Children echo and write

5. Turn to the next lesson.

Old Woman

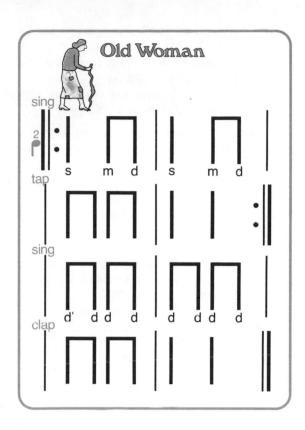

OLD WOMAN

American Folk Song

1. Old Wo - man, old wo - man, Are you fond of card - ing?

Old wo - man, old wo - man, Are you fond of card - ing?

Speak a lit - tle loud - er, sir! I'm ver - y hard of hear - ing.

2. Old woman, old woman,
   Are you fond of spinning? (*Repeat*)
   Speak a little louder, sir!
   I'm very hard of hearing. (*Repeat*)

3. Old woman, old woman,
   Will you darn my stocking? (*Repeat*)
   Speak a little louder, sir!
   I'm very hard of hearing. (*Repeat*)

4. Old woman, old woman,
   Will you let me court you? (*Repeat*)
   Speak a little louder, sir!
   I just begin to hear you. (*Repeat*)

5. Old woman, old woman,
   Don't you want to marry me? (*Repeat*)
   Oh, my goodness gracious me!
   I think that now I hear you!

PREPARATION FOR THE CHART

1. This song was introduced in Level 1, Chart 33. Clap it as a mystery song and see if the children can identify it.
2. Sing the song, and use previous rhythmic experiences. (see Lesson 1.)

INTRODUCE THE CHART

1. Choose one child to read and clap the rhythm pattern with rhythm syllables. Be sure to observe the repeat signs.
2. Choose another child to sing the first line of the chart with hand or arm signals. The class will tap the second line, without losing the beat, using rhythm syllables.

25

3. Review high do (do')—fists raised above head (Chart 32, Level 1).
   - Ask a volunteer to sing the third line with hand or arm signals.
   - The class will read the last line with clapping and rhythm syllables.
4. Read and sing the entire chart with the class, using tone syllables, hand signals, tapping, and clapping.
5. Sing the song with words, hand signals, tapping, and clapping.
6. Use flash cards for inner hearing and vary the rhythmic responses (see Level 1, Chart 3).
   - Choose one child to sing Lines 1 and 3 with tone syllables and hand signals. The class will follow the directions on the flash cards for Lines 2 and 4:

tap	feel	step	clap

   - Be sure to move from line to line without losing the beat.
7. Ask a child to keep the beat on the chart while the class sings the song with hand signals and words.
8. Ask another child to be the conductor while the class sings the song. Be sure to observe the down beat.
9. If the class has learned all the verses, divide the class into two groups:
   - Group 1 sings the "question."
   - Group 2 sings the "old woman."
   - Later, ask two children to perform the part of the "question" and the "old woman."

ADDITIONAL ACTIVITIES

1. *Form—Similarities and Differences*
   - Which phrases are alike and which one is different?
   - Make a picture of the melody in the air with large arm movements (**melodic contour**).
   - Put the picture of the melody on paper or on the chalkboard:

Phrase 1   *Phrase 2*   *Phrase 3*

   - The form can also be shown with letters or geometric shapes:

        A A B or ▲ ▲ ●

2. *Instruments*
   - Read and play the rhythm pattern on the chart with rhythm instruments:
     Phrases 1 and 2—wood block or sticks
     Phrase 3—tambourine or drum
   - Pass out the C–E–G and high C resonator bells. Let the children discover which bells will play the melody.
     "Old Woman"—G–E–C
     "Speak a little louder, sir!"—C'–C–C–C–C–C–C–C
   - This activity can also be done with the recorder, song flute, or song bells.

Note: C–E–G–C' is closest to a child's vocal range, without using sharps or flats.

3. Divide the class into two groups. One group plays instruments, and the other sings the song.
   - Ask one child to act as the conductor for the two groups.
   - Ask one child to play the first beat of each measure on the drum (accent).

EVALUATION OF RHYTHMIC AND PERCEPTUAL SKILLS

Aural Acuity and Perception

1. Can the children recognize and perform duple rhythms?
2. Can they hear and perform the accented beat?
3. Can they recognize the minor third (s–m), perfect fifth (s–d), and octave (d'–d) and reproduce these intervals, either vocally or on an instrument?

Psychomotor Development and Perception

1. Can the children conduct and feel duple rhythms?
2. Can they perform duple rhythms with body motions?
3. Can they feel the phrases and demonstrate melodic similarities and differences with body motions?

What Do You Hear?

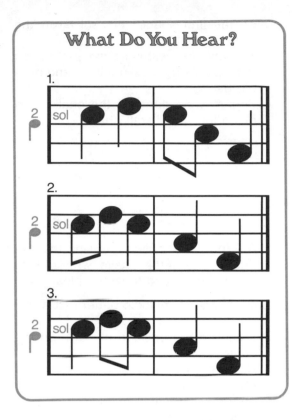

What Do You Hear?

1.

2 sol

2.

2 sol

3.

2 sol

INTRODUCE THE CHART

Note: This chart is a culmination of the two preceding charts.

1. What does the time signature mean ($\frac{2}{4}$)? (two quarter notes or ta's to measure)

2. What does the bar line mean? (the bar line marks the measures into groups of two)

3. What does the double bar tell you? (the double bar indicates the end)

4. What does the top number of any time signature tell you? (the number of beats in a measure)

5. Choose individual children to clap any pattern on the chart. Have the class identify the pattern by raising one, two, or three fingers.

6. Name the tone syllables on the chart, moving from line to line. Do not sing.
   - The children will discover that each line has the same tone syllables, only the rhythm pattern is different.
   - Use hand signals while naming the tone syllables.

7. Sing one of the phrases on the chart, using a neutral syllable such as "loo," and hand signals. The children will identify the phrase by raising the correct number of fingers.

8. Ask someone to sing a phrase on the chart using tone syllables and hand signals. Have the class identify the phrase.
   - If the children are confident, let them establish their own starting pitch. Some children will need assistance.

   - Use many volunteers for this activity. This will give the shy child confidence to perform alone in a game situation rather than singing a solo.

9. The last activity can be used often, not just a part of the music class, but to relieve tensions and provide a break in the school day. Start with Chart 1 and read through the patterns on each chart without losing the beat.

ADDITIONAL ACTIVITIES

1. Sing or play on the bells, piano, or recorder, a melodic pattern using the pentatonic scale and simple duple meter ($\frac{2}{4}$).
   - Establish the position of the starting note on the staff. (For example, "do is

on the first space" or "sol is on the third space.")
- The children will write the pattern on the staff, using measure lines and double bar.
- This may be done on the chalkboard or on individual staff charts.

- Ask individual children to sing the melodic pattern they have written with hand signals and tone syllables.

2. Sing or play a melodic pattern (d s m r d).
   - Establish the position of "do" on the staff.
   - Ask the children to arrange the tones on the chalkboard or on individual charts in as many rhythm patterns as they can think of.
   - Use four beats, two measures, and the double bar:

- Ask individual children to sing their melodic patterns to the class, using tone syllables and hand signals.

3. Choose individual children to sing a melodic pattern of their own, using hand signals and tone syllables. The class will

echo. (Use notes only within the pentatonic scale.) For example,

Leader	Class echoes
l ⊓ l l s l s m d	l ⊓ l l s l s m d
⊓ ⊓ l l d r m s l l	⊓ ⊓ l l d r m s l l
⊓ l ⊓ l l l s m r d	⊓ l ⊓ l l l s m r d
l ⸰ ⊓ l d m s s	l ⸰ ⊓ l d m s s

EVALUATION OF RHYTHMIC AND PERCEPTUAL SKILLS

Aural and Visual Acuity and Perception

1. Can the children recognize and reproduce a simple melodic pattern in duple time?
2. Can they read and sing a simple melodic pattern in duple time?
3. Can they hear a melodic pattern and write the notes on the staff, signifying rhythm patterns and intervals?

Musical Development and Social Maturity

1. Can the children sing their own melodic patterns without being given a starting pitch?
2. Can they perform their own melodic patterns for the class with confidence?

Vertical Scale

Note: There are many children's songs that use the low sol (s,) and low la (l,). The vertical scale shows the relationship to the intervals and their distance from one another. Refer to this chart many times and use it with various activities involving hand singing.

PREPARATION FOR THE CHART

Because Charts 9 and 10 teach the same basic concept, the "Evaluation of Rhythmic and Perceptual Skills" is given at the end of Lesson 10.

1. Teach the following songs.

   Note: The syllable markings are included to assist the teacher.

2. Sing the songs and use previous rhythmic experiences.
   • clap the pattern, step the beat.
   • Sing the song, walk the beat, and turn the phrase.
   • Clap the pattern as a mystery song.

   Note: The children should be familiar with the songs before introducing the chart. This will insure success for both teacher and pupil.

MARY HAD A BABY

Feel two beats   Spiritual

d d d d r m d   s,
1. Ma-ry had a ba-by, Yes, Lord,

d d d d r m d l, s,
Ma-ry had a ba-by, Yes, my Lord,

d d d d r m l s
Ma-ry had a ba-by, Yes, Lord,

m s l l s s d r m r d
The peo-ple keep a-com-ing and the train has gone.

2. What did Mary name him, Yes, Lord,
3. Mary named him Jesus, Yes, Lord,
4. Where was Jesus born, Yes, Lord,
5. Born in lowly stable, Yes, Lord,
6. Where did Mary lay him, Yes, Lord,
7. Laid him in a manger, Yes, Lord,

INTRODUCE THE CHART

This will be the first time the children will see the entire sol–fa scale. The other syllables (fa and ti) will be introduced on later charts with related songs. Fa and ti are the half-steps in the diatonic scale. This can be demonstrated by showing the piano keyboard or a full set of reson-

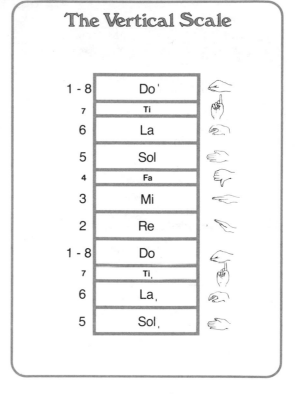

The Vertical Scale

1 - 8	Do'
7	Ti
6	La
5	Sol
4	Fa
3	Mi
2	Re
1 - 8	Do
7	Ti,
6	La,
5	Sol,

ator bells. The half-steps between E and F and B and C will give the children an obvious picture of half-steps without introducing **sharps** (♯) and **flats** (♭).

Half-steps are difficult for children to sing in tune, so the use of the pentatonic scale will enable them to sing the various intervals successfully and then progress to the diatonic scale containing half-steps.

1. Establish the pitch for sol.
2. Place your hand on the sol of the vertical scale, using the hand signal for sol. Sing "sol." Move your hand down to the mi on the vertical scale. Sing the interval of the minor third with tone syllables and hand signals, "sol–mi."

ALL NIGHT, ALL DAY

Refrain

Spiritual

s, d m r d l, d d l, d l, d d l, s,
All night, all day, An-gels watch-ing o-ver me, my Lord,

Fine

s, d m r d s m m d r s, d
All night, all day, An-gels watch-ing o-ver me.

s, l, d r m r m d l, d d l, d l, d d l, s,
Now I lay me down to sleep, An-gels watch-ing o-ver me, my Lord,

D.C. al fine

s, l, d r m r m d s m m d r s, d
Pray the Lord my soul to keep, An-gels watch-ing o-ver me._____

OLD TEXAS

American Cowboy Song

s, d m s l s m d m
1. I'm goin' to leave__ old Tex-as now,

s, d m r m r d s, d
They've got no use____ for the long-horn cow.

2. They've plowed and fenced my cattle range,
And the people there are all so strange.

3. I'll take my horse, I'll take my rope,
And hit the trail upon a lope.

4. Say adios to the Alamo,
And turn my head toward Mexico.

Note: Encourage the children to sit up straight and to breathe deeply so they may hold the tone as long as your hand is on the syllable of the vertical scale. Encourage them to sing each tone with a relaxed jaw, making their mouths look like ◯ for sol and ◠ for mi. Ask the children to make each tone sound as beautiful as they possibly can.

3. On the chart, move your hand slowly from one syllable to another, using hand signals. Sing the intervals that have already been learned with the class, returning to sol to re-establish tonality.

4. Choose one child to make the hand signals on the chart while the class sings the tone syllables with hand signals.

5. Make the hand signals for the first phrase of "Mary Had a Baby" on the chart without singing:

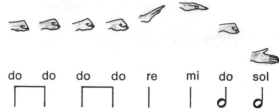

do do do do re mi do sol

- Ask the children to sing your hand signals. Did they recognize the song?
- What happens when they sing "Lord"? (s,)
- Tell the children they have just sung low sol and it is an interval of a perfect fourth.
- Have the children count the steps on the chart from do to sol. How many steps did they count? (4)

6. Sing the second phrase of "Mary Had a Baby" with hand signals on the chart.

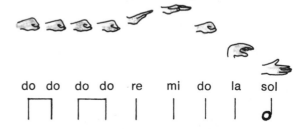

do do do do re mi do la sol

- What syllables did the class sing on "yes, my Lord"? (do–la,–sol,)
- Count the steps down from "do" to la,. How many steps are there? (3)
- Tell the children the interval from "do" to la is a minor third. Some of the children will remember that the interval from sol to mi is also a minor third.

7. Using hand signals on the chart, sing the entire song "Mary Had a Baby" with tone syllables.

8. Present the songs "All Night, All Day" and "Old Texas" at another time, using the same activities.

OTHER SONGS TO USE

These songs can be sung with tone syllables and hand signals on the vertical scale chart.

*   "Camptown Races":

    ⊓ ⊓ ⊓ | ♪ l.   ♪ l.
    s s m s l s m – m r – m r –

*   "Swing Low, Sweet Chariot":

    | ♩ | l. ♪ ⊓ ⁊ ⊓ ⊓ ⊓ | ♩.
    m d m d d l, s, – d d d d m m s s

*   "Get on Board":

    ♪ l. ♩. ⊓ | | ♪ l. ♩ ⊓ | | ♪ l. ♩. ⊓ | | ⁊ | | | ⊓ ♩
    m d l, m m m m r d s, d d d d m d l, d d d d   r m m r r d

ADDITIONAL ACTIVITIES

1. Sing the interval of the minor third and perfect fourth. Use various rhythm patterns and make the hand signals on the chart:

   | | ⊓ | | ⊓ | | | ⊓ | |
   d l, s, s, l,   s, l, l, d m   s m r d l,

2. Divide the class. Tell one group to follow your right hand signals and the other group to follow your left hand signals.

   R.H. s - - l - s - m - - r - - d
   L.H. s - m - r - d - m - s - - l - s - l - s - m - d

   Give individual children an opportunity to lead the class in two-hand singing.

3. Use the vertical scale chart for mystery songs. Make the hand signals on the chart but do not sing. Use only the first phrase of the song. For example,

   "Are You Sleeping?"

   | | | | | | | |
   d r m d, d r m d

   "Michael, Row the Boat"

   | | | l. ⊓ l. ♩ | | ♩   ♩
   d m s m s l s – m s l _____ s ____

   "Dummy Line"

   | | | ⊓ ⊓ | | ⁊
   d d l, s, s, d d d l,

   ⊓ ⊓ ⊓ ⊓ ⊓ ⁊ |
   d d d d m m d d m m   r

4. Turn to the next lesson.

10 Turn the Glasses Over

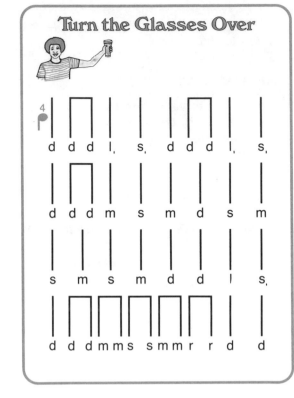

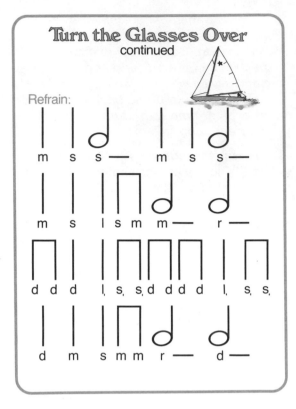

PREPARATION FOR THE CHART

1. Teach the song.
2. Sing the song and use previous rhythmic experiences.

INTRODUCE THE CHART

1. Establish the beat with "One, two, ready, read." Read the rhythm pattern of both charts with rhythm syllables and clapping without losing the beat.
2. Ask one child to be the conductor while you turn the charts.
3. Read the entire song with hand signals and tone syllables but do not sing (inner hearing). Step the beat.
4. Sing the entire song with hand signals and tone syllables. Step the beat.

5. Divide the class into two groups.
   - Group 1 sings the first line of the chart with hand signals and tone syllables.
   - Group 2 sings the second line with hand signals and tone syllables without losing the beat.
   - Continue through both charts, each group singing a line.
6. Divide the class into two groups.
   - Group 1 sings the first line of the chart with words and hand signals, taking four steps forward and four steps backward on the beat.
   - Group 2 sings the second line of the chart with words and hand signals, taking four steps forward and four steps backward on the beat.
   - Continue without losing the beat.

ADDITIONAL ACTIVITIES

1. Create several rhythmic ostinatos to accompany the song. Use some of the patterns contained in the song:

   woodblock
   tambourine
   drum

2. Put the rhythm patterns on the chalkboard.
   - Create a melodic ostinato

     d'   s s l   s

     s, l, s, l,   d m

     l   s

TURN THE GLASSES OVER
American Singing Game

I've been to Haar-lem, I've been to Do-ver,

I've trav-eled this wide world all o - ver,

o - ver, o - ver, three times o - ver,

Drink what you have to drink and

turn the glass - es o - ver.

Refrain

Sail - ing east, sail - ing west,

Sail - ing o - ver the o - cean,

Bet - ter watch out when the boat be-gins to rock,

Or you'll lose your girl in the o - cean.

- Play one of the ostinatos on the reso-nator bells while the class sings the song.
- Try playing several ostinatos while the class sings the song.

3. Create words to one, two, or all three original patterns. Divide the class and sing one ostinato while one group sings the song. For example,

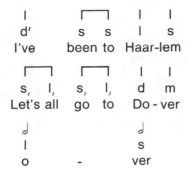

	⌐		
d'	s s		s
I've	been to	Haar-lem

⌐	⌐		
s, l,	s, l,	d m
Let's all	go to	Do-ver

♩		♩
o	-	ver

4. Depending on the musical capabilities of the children, divide the class into two, three, or four groups:
   - Group 1 sings the song
   - Groups 2, 3, and/or 4 sing one or more of the melodic ostinatos.

5. Sing the song and step one of the above rhythm patterns.

6. Teach the dance.
   - Formation: Double circle of partners facing counterclockwise. Hands joined skating fashion, left hands above.
   - Walk the beat while singing the song until "Turn the glasses over." Each couple "wrings the dishrag" (partners raise hands, turn back to back under own arms until they are face to face. Hands remain joined)

- Drop hands, girls continue walking original direction (CCW), boys go the opposite direction (CW).
- On the words "lose your girl," find the closest partner and repeat the dance.

EVALUATION OF RHYTHMIC AND PERCEPTUAL SKILLS

Psychomotor Development and Perception

1. Can the children move freely to the beat?
2. Can they feel the phrase endings and reverse direction while walking the beat (position in space)?

Aural and Visual Acuity and Perception

1. Are the children becoming increasingly confident at identifying various intervals?
2. Are they able to maintain a given melodic pattern while another group is singing?
3. Are they reading the symbols on the charts with growing confidence and little or no assistance from the teacher?
4. Can they identify previously introduced intervals on the vertical scale?

Musical Development and Social Maturity

1. Are the children finding increased enjoy-ment and excitement in producing beau-tiful sounds?
2. Are they becoming increasingly confident while performing individual musical activ-ities?

Where Is Sol,?
Where Is La,?

Low Sol

Low La

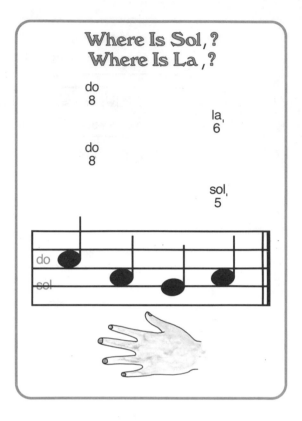

Where Is Sol,?
Where Is La,?

do
8

la,
6

do
8

sol,
5

do

sol

INTRODUCE THE CHART

1. Establish the pitch for "do."
   - Sing do–la, with hand signals.
   - The class echoes do–la, with hand signals.

2. Sing do–sol, with hand signals. The class echoes do–sol, with hand signals.

3. Ask someone in the class to explain the meaning of the numbers 8 and 6 on the chart.

   Note: You may wish to refer to the vertical scale. The "8" refers to the descending interval.

   - How many steps from 8 to 6? (3)
   - What is the name of the interval? (minor third)

4. Ask someone in the class to explain the meaning of the 8 and 5 on the chart.
   - Repeat the above activities.
   - What is the name of the interval? (perfect fourth)

5. Refer to the vertical chart. Ask the children if they have ever sung a minor third or a perfect fourth. (sol–mi minor third and la–mi perfect fourth)

6. Establish the pitch for "do." Create melodic patterns using low la and low sol:

   | | | | | ⌐ | |
   d l, d s,,   d s, s, l, s,

7. Point to the staff on the chart.
   - If "do" is in a space, where is la,? (the space below "do")

- If la, is in a space, where is sol,? (the line below la,)

8. Establish the pitch for "do." Ask several children to sing the notes as you point to the chart. (Do not sing.) Encourage many children to participate in this activity.

9. Use the hand on the chart to vary the position of "do" in relationship to la and sol.
    - If "do" is around the fourth line: where is la,?

    - If "do" is in the fourth space: where Is sol,?

    - Relate this activity to intervals previously learned.

Note: Many songs begin below the staff. The added lines are called ledger lines and will be introduced on a later chart. The ledger lines can be taught by rote at this time.

    - If "do" is in the first space: where is la,?

    Where is sol,?

Note: Use one finger of the left hand to portray the ledger line. The children will relate to the position of the intervals by grasping your finger or placing their fingers in the correct space.

ADDITIONAL ACTIVITIES

1. *Dictation:* Use the chalkboard or individual staff charts. Establish the position of the starting note on the staff (i.e., "do" is in the second space):

Teacher sings with hand signals	Class echoes and writes
⎸ ⎸ ⎸ ⎸ d l, s, l,	
"do is on the fourth line" ⎸ ⎸ ⊓ ⎸ d m d d l,	
"low sol is on the first line" ⎸ ⊓ ⎸ ⎸ s, d r m s	

    - Use many variations of melodic patterns.
    - Ask the children to sing the patterns they have written so the class may correct their own work.

2. Use hand signals but do not sing. Ask individual children to sing your pattern with hand signals.

    Teacher

    Child sings   d l, d s,.

Ask individual children to lead the class in this activity. Most children will be able to establish their own starting pitch.

EVALUATION OF RHYTHMIC AND PERCEPTUAL SKILLS

Musical Development and Social Maturity

1. Can the children understand the concept of low la (l,) and low sol (s,)?
2. Can the children relate the minor third and perfect fourth to previously learned intervals (s–m, l–m)?

Triple Meter

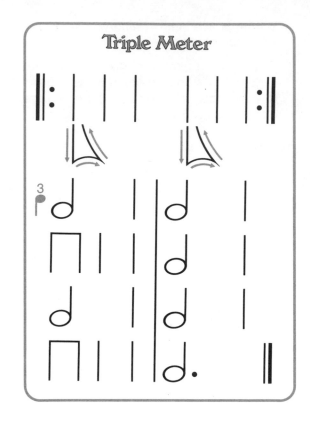

Triple Meter

Note: Charts 12, 13, and 14 all teach the same basic concept, and therefore the "Evaluation" for these charts is given at the end of Lesson 14.

PREPARATION FOR THE CHART

1. Teach the song.
2. Sing the song and step the beat.

   Note: Tell the children to step, tip-toe to get the accent on the first beat. Some children will have difficulty because of the change from right to left:

   R. L. R. L. R. L.
   1 2 3, 1 2 3 etc.

3. Sing the song, step the beat, and clap the first beat of each measure (**accent**).

4. Step the beat, clap the accent, and sing only the accented beat. For example,

   Come - - sing - - song - - three - - etc.

5. Sing the song and walk the beat while clapping the accent.
   - Bend the knees on the first beat and tiptoe on "two" and "three."
   - Change direction at the end of the phrase.

INTRODUCE THE CHART

1. Stand with your back to the class. Ask the children to move their right arm just like yours:
   - On the first beat or downbeat, your arm goes straight down and bounces a bit.

COME, LET'S SING

Words adapted by E. Kidd   French Round

Come, let's sing a song, it is in three four;

Come, let's sing a song in three four time.

- On the second beat, your arm moves to the right.
- On the third beat, your hand moves up, ready to make the next downbeat.

2. Choose individuals to come up to the chart and follow the conducting pattern

for three with their right arm while the class claps the rhythm pattern with syllables at the top of the chart.

3. Ask one child to read and clap the rhythm pattern at the bottom of the chart.
   - What happens in the last measure? Was the dotted note (♩.) held for the full three beats?
   - Did the children identify the song?

4. Tell the children the rule for a dotted note.

Note: The dot gets half the value of the note it comes after.

Put the following on the chalkboard:

𝅝 = 4 beats   𝅝. = 4 + 2 or 6 beats
♩ = 2 beats   ♩. = 2 + 1 or 3 beats

Note: Be sure the children clap the first beat only for the dotted note and shake clasped hands for the silent beats:

   𝅝   clap, shake, shake, shake
   ♩. clap, shake, shake

5. Sing the song, clap the pattern, and step the beat.

6. Choose one child to be the conductor while the class sings the song and claps the pattern.

ADDITIONAL ACTIVITIES

1. Play an instrumental accompaniment to the song:

   woodblock or tambourine: ♩ ⏐ ⏐ ♩ ⏐
   drum or sticks: ⊓ ⏐ ⏐

2. Clap a two- or four-measure pattern in three/four (3/4) time.
   - Children will write the pattern on the chalkboard or individual charts. One measure at a time.
   - After the children have written the pattern, tell them to put in the barlines so each measure contains three beats:

   Teacher dictates with clapping
   ⏐ ⏐ ⏐   ⊓ ⏐ ⏐   ♩.   ⏐ ⏐ ⏐

   Children write
   ⏐ ⏐ ⏐ ⏐ ⊓ ⏐ ⏐ ⏐ ♩. ⏐ ⏐ ⏐ ⏐ ‖

3. Play a recording of a waltz; for example, "Waltz of the Flowers" by Tschaikovsky or "Blue Danube" by Strauss. Ask several children to take turns being the conductor while the class taps the beat on their desks.

4. Place the following patterns on the chalkboard. Have the children tap with their right hands and rap their knuckles on the desk with their left hands.

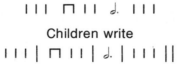

Do this activity and sing "Come, Let's Sing."

5. Turn to the next lesson.

Mystery Songs

PREPARATION FOR THE CHART

1. Teach the songs.
2. Sing the songs and use previous rhythmic activities that apply to 3/4 meter:
   - Clap-tap-tap
   - Step or walk the beat and clap the pattern.
3. Choose one child to conduct the class while they sing one of the songs.
   - Review the anacrusis for "On Top of Old Smoky," making sure the downbeat is on the first beat:

     On | top of old etc.
     3 | 1   2   3

   - Be sure to keep the beat while singing the dotted half-note (♩.) and the tied notes (♩. ♩. ♩.). How many beats does the last note get? (8)

INTRODUCE THE CHART

1. Clap the pattern to one of the songs on the chart.
   - Ask the children to identify the pattern.
   - Can they identify the song?
   - Ask the child who correctly identified the song to conduct while the class sings.
2. Ask for volunteers to read and clap one of the patterns on the chart with rhythm syllables. Have the class identify the pattern on the chart, identify the song, and then sing the song with one child conducting.

OTHER SONGS TO USE

"We Wish You a Merry Christmas" • "Sing Your Way Home" • "The Star Spangled Banner."

ADDITIONAL ACTIVITIES

1. Sing one of the songs and make large arm movements in the air to show the phrases. Mark the phrases on a large piece of paper or on the chalkboard.
2. Sing one of the songs and make the melodic contour on the chalkboard, in the air, or on a large piece of paper. The melodic contour will vary with each child. For example,

SING MUSIC THAT'S GAY

Words by E. Kidd   Italian Folk Song

1. Sing mu - sic that's gay,_____
2. Sing songs that are glad,_____

Sing all through the day,_____
Sing songs that are sad,_____

Life can be mer - ry as we go a - long;
Sing with your heart as you go through the day;

Sing mu - sic that's gay.
Sing songs that are glad.

SKATER'S WALTZ

Words by E. Kidd   E. Waldteufel

1. Ska - ting with me,_____
2. See how we glide,_____

Hearts filled with glee,_____
We're side by side,_____

Fly - ing a - long like a
O - ver the ice as we

bird that's free.
slide, slide, slide.

ON TOP OF OLD SMOKY

Kentucky Folk Song

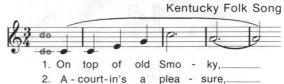

1. On top of old Smo - ky,_____
2. A - court - in's a plea - sure,_____

All cov - ered with snow,_____
A - flirt - in's a grief,_____

I lost my true lov - er,_____
A false heart - ed lov - er

A - cour - tin' too slow.
Is worse than a thief._____

- "Sing Music That's Gay" 〰
- "Skater's Waltz" 〰
- "On Top of Old Smoky" 〰

3. The use of melodic contour can make an interesting art project. Make the contour of each phrase a different color with crayon in heavy, broad strokes on drawing paper. Cover the paper with a watercolor wash.

4. Discuss the appropriate instrumental accompaniment for each song:

   "Sing Music That's Gay"
   tambourine, jingle sticks

"Skater's Waltz"
triangle, jingle bells
"On Top of Old Smoky"
wood block, sticks

5. Ask the children to create a rhythm pattern in 3/4.

♩ | | | ♩ ♫ | | ♫ | |

Play one of the patterns on a rhythm instrument as an ostinato while singing the song. As the class becomes more confident, use two or more ostinatos.

6. Discover which phrases are similar and which are different. Mark the phrases with letter names or geometric figures. For example,

"Sing Music That's Gay"   A B C A
"Skater's Waltz"   ● ▲ ■ ▬
"On Top of Old Smoky"   A–B

7. Turn to the next lesson.

39

There's a Hole in the Bucket

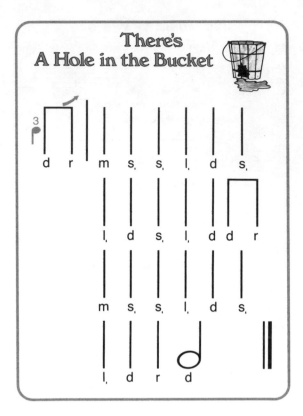

THERE'S A HOLE IN THE BUCKET

American Folk Song

G: There's a hole in the buck - et, dear Li - za, dear Li - za;
L: Mend the hole, then, dear Geor - gie, dear Geor - gie, dear Geor - gie;

G: There's a hole in the buck - et, dear Li - za, a hole.
L: Mend the hole, then, dear Geor - gie, dear Geor - gie, the hole!

G: With what shall I mend it,
L: With a straw, then,

G: If the straw be too long, then,
L: Cut the straw, then,

G: With what shall I cut it,
L: With a knife, then,

G: If the knife be too dull, then,
L: Whet the knife, then,

G: With what shall I whet it,
L: With a stone, then,

G: If the stone be too rough, then,
L: Smoothe the stone, then,

G: With what shall I smooth it,
L: With water,

G: In what shall I fetch it,
L: In a bucket,

(Spoken) There's a hole in the bucket!

PREPARATION FOR THE CHART

1. Teach the song.
2. Sing the song and use previous rhythmic experiences.
3. Stop singing at a given signal but continue the song inwardly. Continue the song at a given signal. Use inner hearing flash cards.

4. Divide the class. Boys sing the part of "Georgie" and girls sing the part of "Liza."

INTRODUCE THE CHART

1. Read and clap the rhythm pattern of the entire chart with the class, using rhythm syllables. Establish the beat, remembering the anacrusis:

      ⊓ | | |

  One, two, ti ti | ta ta ta | etc.

2. Ask one of the children to keep the beat on the chart while the class sings the song and steps the rhythm pattern.
3. Make the hand signals for the song without singing, hearing the melody inside.

Note: Refer to the vertical scale (Chart 9) for space relationship of low sol (s₁) and low la (l₁). Do this activity quite slowly, at first.

4. Sing the entire chart with hand signals and tone syllables.
5. Sing the entire chart with hand signals and words.

ADDITIONAL ACTIVITIES

1. Use flash cards of rhythm patterns in 3/4 meter of two measures.

Move around the room, giving each child an opportunity to clap a pattern.

2. *Dictation:* Clap or tap two-measure patterns in 3/4 meter. Have the children write the pattern or place the rhythm symbols on individual charts, marking the measures:

Teacher dictates   Class echoes and writes

| | | |⊓ | | | | | | | |⊓ | |
            ta   ta   ta|ti–ti ta ta

| ⊓³ || | ≀ || | ⌢³ | | | | ≀ |
         ta triple–ti ta | ta rest ta

As the children become more confident, extend the patterns to four measures.

3. Ask the class to sing "The Skater's Waltz" by phrases.
   - Write the rhythm pattern on paper or the chalkboard.
   - Mark the measure bars.

EVALUATION OF RHYTHMIC AND PERCEPTUAL SKILLS

Aural Acuity and Perception

1. Can the children hear and perform songs in 3/4 meter?
2. Can they hear and differentiate the various note values (| ⊓ ♩.)?
3. Can they identify familiar songs in 3/4 meter by their rhythm pattern?

Visual Acuity and Perception

1. Can the children read various rhythm patterns in 3/4 meter?
2. Can they read the tone syllables on the chart and sing the intervals?

Psychomotor Development and Perception

Can the children feel the triple meter and perform related motor activities such as stepping • walking • swaying?

Musical Development and Social Maturity

1. Can the children feel the phrase of the song?
2. Can they recognize similarities and differences? For example,

    A B C A (form in music)

3. Can they use musical discrimination when playing an instrumental accompaniment to a song?

Read A New Pattern

Note: Charts 15, 16, and 17 all teach the same basic concept, and therefore the "Evaluation" is given at the end of Lesson 17.

PREPARATION FOR THE CHART

1. *Echo clapping.* Give every child an opportunity to clap patterns for the class to echo, using either duple or triple meter.
2. Review the tied note (I_I Chart 46) and the dotted note (♩. Chart 12).

   Note: Remember, both the tied note and the dotted note are clapped and held for the silent beat (ta–a). The dot gets half the value of the note it comes after.

INTRODUCE THE CHART

1. Point to the first line of the chart. Tell the class that sometimes the eighth note (ti) is separated and used by itself (♪).
2. Read and clap the first two lines of the chart with rhythm syllables, stepping the beat.
3. Ask for volunteers to clap lines 3, 4, 5, and 6 of the chart. Many children will be able to read the pattern successfully if they have been given sufficient background on previous rhythms.
4. Step the beat, and read and clap the entire chart with rhythm syllables. Set a fairly slow tempo for the first reading.
5. Divide the class into two groups.

- Group 1 claps the first two beats of the chart with rhythm syllables.
- Group 2 echoes.
- Keep the beat on the chart as you move from line to line. Later, let the children read the chart unassisted or with a student leader.

ADDITIONAL ACTIVITIES

1. Sing "Old Woman" (Chart 7) and clap one line of the chart as an ostinato. Step the beat while singing the song and clapping the pattern.
2. When the children become more confident, sing the song and clap the entire

chart as an accompaniment. Read and clap the chart with any familiar song that is in duple meter (2 or 4).

3. Dictate various patterns using the single eighth notes and dotted quarters. Write the patterns on paper or individual rhythm charts.

Teacher claps
or taps   Class echoes   Class writes

♪ ♪ ♪ ┃ ┃   ti ta ti ta ta   ♪ ♪ ♪ ┃ ┃

┃. ♪ ┃. ♪   ta-a ti ta-a ti   ┃. ♪ ┃. ♪

4. Make flash cards of various patterns, using syncopation. Move from child to child in order to give everyone an opportunity to read and clap a pattern:

5. Play one line of the chart as an instrumental ostinato to a familiar song such as "Yankee Doodle," "I've Been to Haarlem," or "Are You Sleeping?"

6. Create a melody to the rhythm pattern:

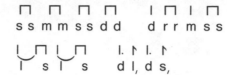

ss m m ss d d   d r r m ss

┃. ♪ ┃. ♪
l   s l   s   d l, d s,

Let the children decide which intervals will create the better melody by singing what they have written.

7. Encourage the children to write words to their melody.

Note: You may wish to put some of the better original songs on a large chart for future use.

8. Tell the class they have just accomplished a very important musical activity and that they can add a new word to their musical vocabulary:

Syncopation: a deliberate change of the normal beat or meter.

Note: Syncopation has been used by many great composers in order to create exciting rhythms. The children will probably be more familiar with jazz, which is a true American musical idiom and is based primarily on syncopated rhythms.

9. Turn to the next lesson.

Mystery Songs

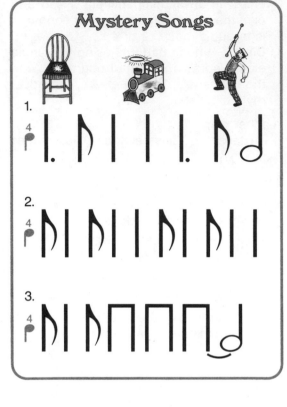

PREPARATION FOR THE CHART

1. Teach the songs.
2. Sing the songs and use previous rhythmic experiences.

Chairs to Mend

- Divide the class into three groups and sing the song as a round while stepping the beat.
- Try stepping or walking the pattern as a round while in three groups, changing direction on each phrase.

Mr. Banjo

- Sing the song and march the beat. How would "Mr. Banjo" walk if he were leading a parade? (prance)

This Train

- Sing the song and step the pattern while clapping the beat.
- How many steps did the class take to the beat when they sang "nothin" but the"? (4)
- The sixteenth note will be developed further on a later chart.

INTRODUCE THE CHART

1. Clap one of the patterns on the chart and have the children identify which line it is by holding up the correct number of fingers.
2. Choose one child to clap a pattern on the chart for the class to identify. Sing the songs after they have been identified.

3. Read each line of the chart with clapping and rhythm syllables.

OTHER SONGS TO USE

"America, the Beautiful"

"Erie Canal"

"Above the Plain"

These songs can be used as mystery songs.

ADDITIONAL ACTIVITIES

1. "Chairs to Mend":
   - Divide the class into three groups. Let

each group decide which sound they will use. For example,

Group 1: clap
Group 2: tap
Group 3: rap on desk

Note: This activity can be performed on rhythm instruments.

- Ask a small group of children to sing an ostinato to the round:

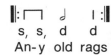

s, s, d d
An-y old rags

- Encourage the children to create original ostinatos, using rhythms, melody, and words.

2. "Mr. Banjo":

- Create several rhythmic ostinatos to play on instruments while the class sings the song:

Maracas or tambourine: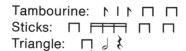
Claves or sticks:
Drum:

3. "This Train":

- Select a rhythm pattern from the song to play on instruments while the class sings the song.

Tambourine:
Sticks:
Triangle:

4. Turn to the next lesson.

CHAIRS TO MEND

Traditional Round

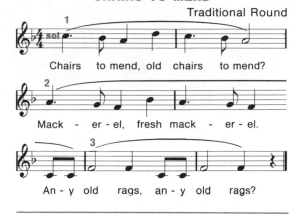

Chairs to mend, old chairs to mend?

Mack - er - el, fresh mack - er - el.

An - y old rags, an - y old rags?

MR. BANJO

Creole Song

1. Look at our lead - er, see Mis - ter Ban - jo,
2. He is our lead - er, see Mis - ter Ban - jo,

Twirl - ing that big ba - ton, Mis - ter Ban - jo,
Hold - ing his chin up high, Mis - ter Ban - jo,

Lead - ing us down the street, Mis - ter Ban - jo,
Wear - ing a bright red tie, Mis - ter Ban - jo,

March - ing with lift - ed feet!
Un - der a hat so high!

THIS TRAIN

American Folk Song

1. This train is bound for glo - ry, This train,—

This train is bound for glo - ry, This train—

This train is bound for glo - ry,

Don't rid no - thin' but the good and ho - ly,

This train is bound for glo - ry, This train.—

2. This train don't pull no extras, This train, (*Repeat*)
Don't pull nothin' but the midnight special,

3. This train don't pull no jokers, This train, (*Repeat*)
Neith-er don't pull no 'seegar' smokers,

4. This train don't pull no sleepers, This train, (*Repeat*)
Don't pull nothin' but the righteous people,

Canoe Song

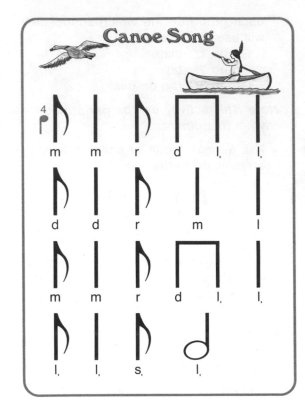

PREPARATION FOR THE CHART

1. Teach the song.
2. Sing the song and use previous rhythmic experiences.
   - Step the beat and clap the pattern.
   - Clap the beat and step the pattern.
   - Use inner hearing. Repeat the song several times and use inner hearing flash cards.

3. Sing the song as a two-part round.
4. Step the song as a two-part round.

INTRODUCE THE CHART

1. Point to the chart and read and clap the rhythm pattern with rhythm syllables. Step the beat.
2. Read the chart and step the rhythm pattern while clapping the beat.
3. Make the hand signals for the song without singing. Keep the tempo quite slow until the children become confident.

   Note: Observe the distance of the intervals as the children make the hand signals, especially low la (l,), low sol (s,), and the interval of mi–la.

4. Sing the chart with tone syllables and hand signals. Step the beat.

5. Sing the song with hand signals and words.
6. Divide the class. Have one group step the beat, while the other groups sing the song as a two-part round.

ADDITIONAL ACTIVITIES

1. Choose a small group of children to sing the last measure of the song as an ostinato while the rest of the class sings the song as a two-part round:

   dip, dip, and swing: ♪ | ♪ ♩

2. Sing the song as a two-part round, repeating the song several times.

46

CANOE SONG

American Indian Song

1. My pad-dle's keen and bright, flash-ing with sil-ver
2. Dip, dip and swing her back, flash-ing with sil-ver

Fol-low the wild goose flight, dip, dip and swing.
Fol-low the wild goose flight, dip, dip and swing.

- Begin singing very softly (pp), as if the canoe is far away.
- Gradually get louder (<), as the canoe gets closer (f).
- Gradually get softer (>), as the canoe paddles away.
- Review the musical terms for dynamics and their signs:

    crescendo <
    decrescendo >
    pianissimo pp
    forte f

3. Create an instrumental accompaniment by using one of the measures in the song:

    drum ♪ I ♪ I I
    sticks ♪ I ♪ ⊓ I

4. Write a four-measure pattern on the chalkboard using syncopation, or use four rhythm flash cards consecutively:

- Ask one child to read and clap the entire pattern with rhythm syllables.
- The class will echo.
- Divide the class and read the four measures as a canon.
- Use the repeat sign and clap the pattern as a canon.

5. Let the children experiment with the black notes on the piano or resonator bells until they can play the melody of the "Canoe Song."

EVALUATION OF RHYTHMIC AND PERCEPTUAL SKILLS

Aural Acuity and Perception

1. Can the children clap a syncopated pattern without losing the beat?
2. Are they singing intervals using low sol (s,) and low la (l,) with increasing confidence?

Visual Acuity and Perception

1. Can the children read a syncopated pattern with ease and confidence?
2. Can they read extended rhythm patterns?
3. Can they read a rhythm pattern and identify a familiar song?
4. Can they recognize the symbol for the single eighth note (♪) and clap or sing the pattern correctly?

Octaves

Octaves

Note: Because Charts 18 and 19 both teach the same basic concept, the "Evaluation" for these charts is given at the end of Lesson 19.

PREPARATION FOR THE CHART

1. Review the vertical scale (Chart 9). Establish the pitch for sol and sing various patterns with hand signals on the chart, using tone syllables. The class will echo:

Teacher sings	Class echoes
I ⊓ I I	I ⊓ I I
s m r d d'	s m r d d'
⊓ I I I	⊓ I I I
m r d l, s,	m r d l, s,
I I ⊓ I	I I ⊓ I
d m s l d'	d m s l d'

2. Establish the pitch.
   • Make hand signals on the Vertical Scale Chart *without* singing, using **octaves.**
   • The class will sing the pattern with tone syllables and hand signals:

Teacher signals on chart	Class sings
I I ⊓ I	I I ⊓ I
s s, s s s,	s s, s s s,
I ⊓ I I	I ⊓ I I
I l,l, I I,	I l,l, I I,

   • Ask one child to be the leader for this activity

3. Introduce the prefix "oct."
   • How many arms does an octopus have? (8)
   • How many sides does an octagon have? (8)
   • How many steps on the vertical scale from do to do' or sol to sol'? (8)

INTRODUCE THE CHART

Note: This will be an introduction to ledger lines. These are short lines drawn above or below the staff. The class will note that if one note is on a line (do), the upper octave will be on a space (do').

1. Ask the children to clap the pattern while you keep the beat on the chart. Step the beat while clapping the pattern.
2. Point to the chart and make the arm signals in rhythm without singing, slowly

48

moving from line to line. Use inner hearing while making the arm signals.

3. Sing the entire chart slowly with arm signals.
   - As the pattern is sung from do to do', the arms swing straight up with clenched fists.
   - When you drop to la, the arms are arched at shoulder level and swing backwards for low la (la,).
   - Going from low la to low sol, clap the hands at chest level and then behind the back.

4. Read and sing the chart several times with arm signals. With each repeat, increase the tempo.

Note: Keep the voices fairly soft. The tendency will be to sing the upper notes too loud.

5. Read and sing the chart with vigorous arm signals and step the beat.

6. Turn to the next lesson.

The Classical Symphony

The Classical Symphony

by
Sergei Prokofiev

Note: In order to use this chart you will need a recording of "The Classical Symphony." Contact the Music Department for assistance in finding the record.

PREPARATION FOR THE CHART

1. Tell the class about Sergei Prokofiev. He was born in Russia in 1891 and died in 1953, so he can be considered a modern composer. Prokofiev's mother played the piano and gave him his first music lessons. When he was thirteen he entered the St. Petersburg Conservatory and began to make a name for himself by using harmonies that were strange to the ear. When he was twenty-three years old, he received a prize as a pianist. Prokofiev was a very hard worker and produced symphonies, operas, concertos, sonatas, music for films, and children's music. Perhaps his most famous composition for children is "Peter and the Wolf."

   The design of the symphony was developed by Haydn, Mozart, and other composers of the Classical Period. Prokofiev used the same design for his *Classical Symphony* but made each section of the composition shorter than the typical symphonic form. The third movement or section of a symphony is usually a dance that has three beats to a measure, like a minuet, but Prokofiev decided to use an old dance form called a "gavotte," which has four beats to the measure.

2. After the children have been told about Sergei Prokofiev, the composer, play a recording of the "Gavotte" from the *Classical Symphony*.

3. Clap the beat and decide whether it is in three or four. Does the composition have an anacrusis? (yes)

INTRODUCE THE CHART

1. Read and clap the pattern with rhythm syllables. How many beats are in the anacrusis? (2)

   Note: Tell the children this pattern is typical of the gavotte.

2. Play the first section of the recording and tap the rhythm pattern while the music is playing.

- Ask the children to tap the rhythm pattern and show when the octave moves from high to low (i.e., right to left).
- What happens to the octave in the second phrase? The octave moves from low to high (left to right).

3. Play the entire "Gavotte."
   - Tap the rhythm pattern, showing the octaves, as before.
   - When the opening theme is repeated, tap the pattern, showing the direction of the octaves.

4. For the more musically capable children, step the pattern on the chart and show the octaves with large arm movements, up or down.

ADDITIONAL ACTIVITIES

1. Establish the position of the beginning note and dictate various melodic patterns using octaves. Use intervals involving ledger lines as introduced in the previous chart. This activity can be done on staff paper or individual staff charts:

Teacher sings or plays
"do" on the first line

⊓ | | |
d m s d′ d

Class echoes with hand signals
and then writes

EVALUATION OF RHYTHMIC AND PERCEPTUAL SKILLS

Aural and Visual Acuity and Perception

1. Can the children hear and recognize the interval of an octave?
2. Can they recognize the octave on the staff and sing the interval?

6/8 Meter

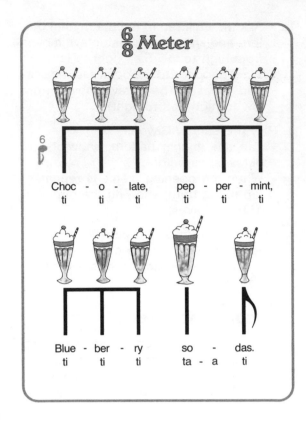

Note: The use of 6/8 meter is very common in western music and is used a great deal in children's songs. Charts 20 through 25 will develop this concept and the "Evaluation" will follow Lesson 25.

PREPARATION FOR THE CHART

1. Charts 20, 21, and 22 introduce six beats to a measure. Show the children that the time signature at the beginning of each chart tells them there are six eighth notes (ti's) in each measure.
2. Give the children a simple rule regarding time signatures:

   "The top number of the time signature tells how many beats in the measure. The bottom number tells what kind of a note gets one beat."

Note: Some children may be interested in seeing how many different time signatures they can find in their music books ($\frac{3}{8}, \frac{5}{4}, \frac{2}{2}$, etc.).

3. The question may arise that 6/8 time looks like "triple–ti." Explain that the triple–ti is used when the three sounds are performed to one beat.

Note: The quarter note (ta) gets two beats because the beat note is an eighth note (ti).

INTRODUCE THE CHART

1. Read and clap the chart, using rhythm syllables. Use a fairly slow tempo at first.
2. Read and clap the chart again, using the words. Accent the first syllable of each word:

   Choc-o-late, pep-per-mint, blue-ber-ry, so-das.

3. Read the chart with words, step the pattern, and clap the accented syllable. How many times did the children clap to each measure? (2)

Note: Tell the children they are clapping a compound meter because each word has a feeling of three but the accent or pulse is in two.

4. Read and clap the chart again at a faster tempo, using the words. Step the accent.
5. Turn to the next lesson.

More 6/8 Meter

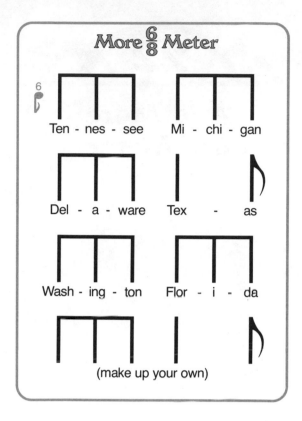

More 6/8 Meter

Ten - nes - see   Mi - chi - gan

Del - a - ware   Tex - as

Wash - ing - ton   Flor - i - da

(make up your own)

INTRODUCE THE CHART

1. Read and clap the pattern.
2. Read and clap the words.
   - Ask the children to find the names of states that will fit the pattern of the last line of the chart:

   I - o - wa,   U - tah,
   O - re - gon, Geor-gia

3. Read the chart again at a faster tempo and step the duple accent.
4. Turn to the next lesson.

And More
6/8 Meter

INTRODUCE THE CHART

1. Read and clap the pattern with rhythm syllables.

   Note: When the children come to the end of line two, tell them that the dotted quarter note (♩.) gets the same number of beats as a dotted half-note (𝅗𝅥.) would get in duple time.

   ♩. ta–a–a, clap, squeeze, squeeze

2. Read the chart and clap the words. Find names of fruits or vegetables that fit the pattern of lines two and four, for example,

cu-cum-ber, squash,
horse-rad-ish, beans

3. Read the chart again at a faster tempo and step the accent, making sure the dotted quarter note is given its full time.

4. Return to Chart 20, and read through to Chart 22 without losing the beat, flipping the pages gently but quickly.
   • Clap the pattern with either rhythm syllables or words and step the accent.
   • Point to the accented beats with one hand while you turn the pages with the other.

ADDITIONAL ACTIVITIES

1. Read a familiar poem or nursery rhyme that has 6/8 meter (e.g., "Pop! Goes the Weasel," "Mulberry Bush," or "Jack and Jill".
   • Read the rhyme to the children, one line at a time.
   • Have the children echo with clapping and rhythm syllables.
   • Write the rhythm symbols on paper. For example,

   | ♪ | ♪
   Jack be nim-ble,
   | ♪ |.
   Jack be quick,
   | ♪ ⊓
   Jack, jump o-ver the
   | ♪ |.
   Can-dle stick

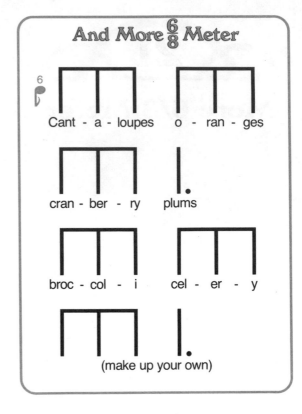

And More ⁶⁄₈ Meter

Cant - a - loupes   o - ran - ges

cran - ber - ry   plums

broc - col - i   cel - er - y

(make up your own)

   • Tell the children to count each measure to make sure there are six beats.

2. *Echo Clapping in Six.* (This activity can also be done with flash cards):

Teacher or Leader	Class echoes and claps
⊓ ⊓ | ♪	♪	⊓ ⊓ | ♪	♪

3. Turn to the next lesson.

Let's Read 6/8 Meter

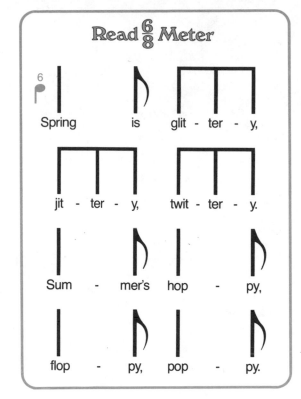

Read 6/8 Meter

Spring   is   glit - ter - y,

jit - ter - y,   twit - ter - y.

Sum - mer's hop - py,

flop - py, pop - py.

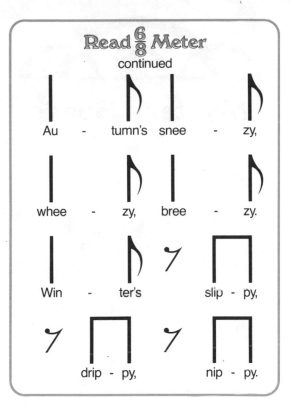

Read 6/8 Meter
continued

Au - tumn's snee - zy,

whee - zy, bree - zy.

Win - ter's slip - py,

drip - py, nip - py.

INTRODUCE THE CHART

1. Read the poem with the class. The children will enjoy the alliteration. Keep the beat in two.
2. Read and clap both charts with rhythm syllables.

   *Note: The two lines at the bottom of Chart 23b introduce the **eighth rest** (⁊), which is the silent beat for ti. Tell the children to make a small rest motion and catch a short quiet breath for the eighth rest. For example,*

   Winter's (catch breath) slippy (ti–ti) etc.

3. Read Chart 23b again with words. This time, instead of catching a breath, feel the eighth rest.
4. Read and clap both charts with rhythm syllables without losing the beat. Increase the tempo, step the duple beat, clap the pattern, and feel the eighth rest.

5. Repeat the last activity, using the words.
6. Go back to Chart 20, and read and clap all five charts with rhythm syllables.

   Note: Keep the duple beat on the charts and do not lose the beat as you move from chart to chart.

7. Repeat the last activity with one child acting as the conductor, using the conducting pattern for two (Chart 6).
8. Turn to the next lesson.

55

Mystery Songs

PREPARATION FOR THE CHART

1. Teach the songs.
2. Sing the songs, using previous rhythmic experiences.
   - Step the duple beat and clap the pattern.
   - Clap the duple beat and step the pattern.

INTRODUCE THE CHART

1. Clap one of the patterns for the children to identify.
   - When the pattern is identified, ask the children if they can identify the song.
   - Ask the child who correctly identified the song to lead the class while they sing the song.

2. Continue with the other patterns on the chart.
   - Wherever possible, give individual children the opportunity to lead the class.
   - As the children become more confident, let the individual children read the charts without assistance.
   - Ask one child to lead the class as they sing one of the songs, establishing the pitch and conducting in duple time.

OTHER SONGS TO USE

Put the rhythm pattern of other familiar songs on the chalkboard, using the first two or three measures. For example,

"Over the River"

ROW, ROW, ROW YOUR BOAT

Traditional Round

Row, row, row your boat gent-ly down the stream,

Mer-ri-ly, mer-ri-ly, mer-ri-ly, mer-ri-ly,

Life is but a dream.

NIGHT HERDING SONG

American Cowboy Song

Oh, slow up, dog-ies, stop rov-ing a-round

I'm tired of your ro - vin' all o - ver the ground;

Oh, graze a-long, dog-ies, and feed kind - a slow,

You don't have for - ev - er to be on the go.

Move slow lit - tle dog-ies, move slow,

Hi - o, hi - o - o, hi - o!

After the children have written the pattern, ask them to put in the measure bars:

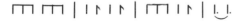

Note: Be sure the children are familiar with a song before using its pattern for identification.

"When Johnny Comes Marching Home," "Little Tom Tinker," and "Lovely Evening" can also be used with this activity.

SING TOGETHER

English Round

Sing, sing to-geth-er, Mer-ri - ly, mer-ri - ly sing;

Sing, sing to-geth - er, Mer-ri - ly, mer-ri - ly sing;

Sing, ___ sing, ___ sing, ___ sing! ___

ADDITIONAL ACTIVITIES

Row, Row, Row Your Boat

1. Sing the song and clap a rhythmic ostinato while stepping the duple beat (x on the music shows duple beat):

    l. l. or ⊓ ⊓ or l ♩ l ♩

2. Play a rhythmic ostinato on an instrument while the class sings the song. For example,

    sticks l. l.   sandblocks l ♩ l ♩

3. Divide the class into three or four groups and sing the song as a round. Tap or step the duple beat while singing the round.

4. Sing the song as a round and choose a small group to sing a melodic ostinato on do and sol. Create words for the ostinato.

Note: Start the ostinato before the class sings the song.

Night Herding Song

1. Sing the song, walk the duple beat, and clap a pattern. Accent the first and third

beat. For example,

    l ♩ l ♩

2. Sing the song and play an instrumental ostinato, using sticks, woodblocks, or coconut shells. Use a pattern contained in the song for the ostinato.

3. Create a melodic ostinato. Let the children decide which syllables to sing with the pattern:

    l ♩ l ♩
    d s, l, s,

- Create words to this melody such as:

    l ♩ l ♩
    I'm a cow - boy
    d s, l, s,

- Divide the class in half and have one group sing the song and the other sing the ostinato.

Sing Together

1. Divide the class into three groups and sing the song as a three-part round.

2. Form three concentric circles.

- Sing the song as a round, walk the duple beat, and change direction on each phrase. Group 1 begins singing the song, walking in one direction and reverses at the end of the first phrase. At this point, Group 2 begins walking and singing. When they reach the end of the first phrase, Group 3 begins. Do not start walking until ready to sing.

Group 1
Group 2
Group 3

3. Choose a small group to sing a melodic ostinato while the rest of the class sings the song as a round.

4. Turn to the next lesson.

The Echo

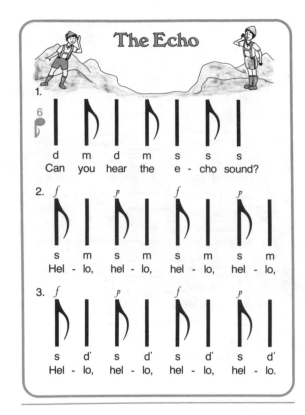

PREPARATION FOR THE CHART

1. Teach the song.
2. Sing the song, step or walk the duple beat (shown by x on the music), and clap the pattern.
3. Use inner hearing flash cards, changing the activity on each phrase.

INTRODUCE THE CHART

1. Establish the beat (one, two, ready, clap). Read the chart with clapping and rhythm syllables.
2. Do the children remember what the *f* and *p* mean on the chart? (*f*—forte or loud; *p*—piano or soft)
3. Read the chart again with clapping and rhythm syllables; observe the dynamic markings.

Note: The success of this activity will depend on the psychomotor ability of the children. Start with a fairly slow tempo to insure success.

4. Read the chart with hand signals but *do not sing*.
5. Establish the pitch for "do" and sing the chart with hand signals and tone syllables. Did the children observe the dynamic markings?
6. Read and sing the chart with words and hand signals. Step the duple beat while singing the song.
7. Divide the class into three groups and sing the song as a round. Use hand signals and repeat the song several times.

Note: You may wish to choose three children to conduct the duple meter for their group.

THE ECHO
Traditional German Song

58

8. Choose three of the more musically capable children to sing the round with hand signals.
9. Starting with Chart 20, clap the pattern with rhythm syllables, moving from chart to chart without losing the beat.

ADDITIONAL ACTIVITIES

1. Use the C–E–G–C' resonator bells and let one child work out the melody of the song. Give several children the opportunity to play the bells while the class sings the song.
2. Sing the song as a three-part round. After all three groups are singing, give the signal to hold the note they are singing. You can stop on any word, but the vowel sound will be more musical. Give another signal to continue the song. What did the children hear when they held the tone? (A chord or triad, which means three or more tones sounded simultaneously)
3. Dictate a two-measure pattern in 6/8 meter. Tell the children to write the pattern on individual staff cards or staff paper and mark the measures, making sure there are six beats in each measure:

Teacher claps or taps	Class echoes and writes

I ♪ I ♪|⎍⎍ I. I   ♪ I   ♪|⎍⎍ I.
                  ta–a ti ta–a ti ti–ti–ti ta–a–a

I. I. |⎍⎍ ⎍⎍ I.   I. |⎍⎍ ⎍⎍
                  ta–a–a ta–a–a ti–ti–ti ti–ti–ti

4. Use flash cards with two-measure 6/8 patterns:

Move from one child to another without losing the beat, giving each child an opportunity to clap a pattern individually.

EVALUATION OF RHYTHMIC AND PERCEPTUAL SKILLS

Psychomotor Development and Perception

Can the children feel the compound meter—triple and duple—with clapping, stepping, and other motor activities?

Aural and Visual Acuity and Perception

1. Can the children identify a familiar song in 6/8 meter?
2. Can they hear and recognize the compound meter?
   • six beats and two pulses.
3. Can they read a pattern in 6/8 with confidence and ease?
4. Can they write various patterns in 6/8 meter?

Social Maturity and Musical Development

1. Can the children approach a new musical concept with confidence?
2. Can they approach a new concept on a chart independently, with little or no assistance from the teacher?

What Meter Do You Hear?

What Meter Do You Hear?

1.

2.

3.

Note: This chart will provide a culmination of the various meter signatures introduced thus far.

PREPARATION FOR THE CHART

Present each line of the chart as an individual rhythm exercise before singing the tone syllables. (Note that each melody is identical except for the rhythmic variations.)

INTRODUCE THE CHART

1. Establish the beat. Read and clap the first line of the chart with rhythm syllables. Which note is the beat note? (ta or quarter note)
2. Continue the beat at the same tempo by tapping the desk.

- Read and clap the pattern for line two. What is the beat note for Line 2? (ti or eighth note)
- How many beats does ta-a or the quarter note get? (2)

3. Read and clap Line 3 at the same tempo. How many beats does the ta-a or half-note get? (2)
4. Ask one child to clap one of the patterns on the chart. Have the class identify the line by raising one, two, or three fingers. Continue through the chart, giving individual children an opportunity to clap a pattern for the class to identify.
5. Tap the beat on the desk. Ask the children to read and clap the entire chart with rhythm syllables, maintaining the same tempo.

Note: Moving from 2/4 to 6/8 to 3/4 meter is a highly integrated activity and may present problems for some of the children.

6. Read the tone syllables of each line with hand signals, but *do not sing.* Let the children discover that the melody is the same and only the rhythm pattern is different.
7. Ask the children to keep the beat on their desks while you sing one of the patterns on the chart with hand signals.
   - Can the class identify which line you sang?
   - Choose individuals to sing one of the melodies on the chart for the class to identify.

Note: Return to this chart several times to give as many children as possible a chance to read and sing one of the patterns.

ADDITIONAL ACTIVITIES

1. Put a melody on the chalkboard without a definite rhythm. For example,

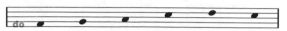

Ask the children to use these tones to make different rhythm patterns in two, three, four, or six beats, using individual staff charts or staff paper.

How many variations can they make? Ask the children to sing their melodies for the class.

EVALUATION OF RHYTHMIC AND PERCEPTUAL SKILLS

Aural Acuity and Perception

1. Can the children hear the differences between duple and triple meters?
2. Can they hear a melodic pattern and identify the meter?

Visual Acuity and Perception

1. Can the children read a rhythm pattern and identify the meter?
2. Can they write rhythm patterns using various meters?

Leader-Echo

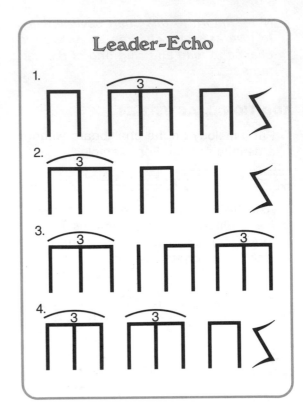

Note: Charts 27, 28, and 29 all teach the same basic concept, and therefore the "Evaluation" is given at the end of Lesson 28.

PREPARATION FOR THE CHART

Note: Echo and canon clapping can be the source of great enjoyment to the children. The ability to listen and concentrate will be greatly enhanced by the use of this rhythmic activity and will also have a direct carry-over to other learnings within the curricula.

1. Begin the canon as you would a round.

Clap or tap a four-beat rhythm pattern and continue with various patterns. The class will always be one measure behind the leader. If the children are insecure, put a four-measure pattern on the chalkboard and approach the canon visually. Later, use canon clapping as an aural rhythm activity.

2. The children should have many opportunities to lead the class in echo and canon clapping. Vary the tone quality of each part by tapping a book, tapping a pencil, rapping the knuckles on a desk, etc.

INTRODUCE THE CHART

1. Choose one child to lead the class. Read and clap the first line of the chart with rhythm syllables. Tell the class to echo only if the pattern is clapped correctly. Continue through the entire chart without losing the beat.
2. Have the class clap the pattern while they step the beat. Choose one child to clap the echo. Repeat the chart several times to give other children an opportunity to echo the pattern.
3. Ask the class to watch the chart carefully and echo *only* if you clap a rhythmic pattern that is on the chart.
4. Use various motor activities for each pattern. The children must echo the sound and the activity.
   - Step the pattern, tap on various objects, etc.
   - Sing one of the patterns on the chart with hand signals for the class to echo:

d m s s s l s

5. Ask for volunteers to lead the class, varying the sound for each pattern.

6. Divide the class into two or more groups, depending on their rhythmic capabilities. Tell the children how many times the chart is to be repeated and clap the chart as a canon. Begin with two parts and let each group decide which tone quality or sound they are going to use.
7. This activity can be done with rhythm instruments.
   - Choose four children to play the chart as a canon.
   - Repeat the chart several times so that each of the four children will have an opportunity to play.
8. Turn to the next lesson.

Chorus–Solo

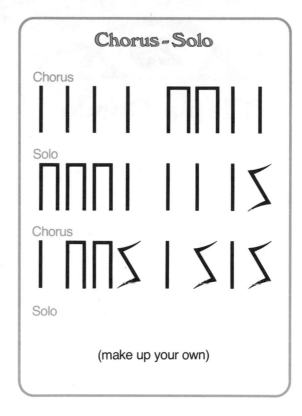

Chorus–Solo

Chorus

Solo

Chorus

Solo

(make up your own)

Note: Choose individual children to read and clap the solo part, using rhythm syllables. The second solo (Line 4 of the chart) must always have the same number of beats as the previous patterns (8), but may use an entirely different rhythm pattern. At first the child may be hesitant to create an original pattern and will probably echo what they have just heard.

INTRODUCE THE CHART

1. Have the class clap the chorus part and have individual children read and clap the solo part. On the last beat of the chorus part, call out someone's name to clap the solo part.

Note: The impetus of the beat will many times overcome the hesitancy on the part of the child.

2. Tell the soloists to use a different sound and pattern from the chorus (e.g., chorus claps, soloist taps; chorus raps desk, soloist claps). This activity should be carried on frequently, not only in the music class.

Note: With repetition the children will feel free to improvise rhythm patterns with confidence, leading to true creativity.

3. Turn to the next lesson.

Clap a Rondo

Clap a Rondo

A. Chorus

B. Solo (make up your own)

A. Chorus

C. Solo (make up your own)

A. Chorus

---

*Note: A **rondo** is an old musical form which dates back as early as the 14th and 15th centuries. The form consists of a main theme (A) alternating with contrasting themes (B and C, etc.). An example might be:*

A – B – A – C – A – etc.

● ■ ● ▲ ●

PREPARATION FOR THE CHART

The rondo form is often used as the last movement of a symphony, and today many jazz groups use the rondo form for improvisation. For example,

A: Main theme—entire group
B: Improvisation—solo
A: Main theme (perhaps altered)—entire group
C: Improvisation—solo; etc.

INTRODUCE THE CHART

1. Tell the class to watch the chart closely because you are going to choose someone to **improvise** the solo part. This child will create an original rhythm pattern with eight beats.

   Note: If the children feel insecure, assign the solo parts to volunteers before the class begins clapping the chorus. This will give the child an opportunity to prepare for his solo.

   Establish the beat and have the class read and clap the rhythm pattern of the chorus part with rhythm syllables.
   - The solo part must enter without losing the beat.
   - The chorus must enter immediately after the soloist.

2. Ask the children to give letter names for each part. If the chorus is A, what letter could be used for the solo? (B)

   Note: Be sure and tell the class that a

rondo can have as many parts as the composer wishes.

3. Assign rhythm instruments for the improvised solo part. For example,

   Class claps for A; Soloist plays woodblock for B; Class claps for A • Second soloist plays tambourine for C; Class claps for A • Third soloist plays triangle for D; Class claps for A; etc.

ADDITIONAL ACTIVITIES

1. Put a two-measure rhythm pattern on the chalkboard:

   Ask the children to write a two-measure pattern on paper or on individual charts, using a different pattern:

   Now have the class clap the pattern on the chalkboard (A), and give each child an opportunity to read and clap his pattern as the soloist. Keep the beat constant as you move from chorus to soloist.

2. For the more musically capable class, put tone syllables to the pattern on the chalkboard. For example,

   - Sing the pattern with tone syllables and hand signals.
   - Tell the children to put tone syllables to their original patterns. Give each child an opportunity to read his melody silently with hand signals and inner hearing.
   - Begin the rondo at a fairly slow tempo, singing the melodic pattern on the chalkboard with hand signals (A).

- Ask several children to sing their original melodic patterns with hand signals (B, C, D, etc.).

Note: Not every child in the class will be successful with this activity but it will prove exciting and challenging to those children with musical ability and talent.

3. Go back to Chart 27, and read all three charts without losing the beat. Choose the soloists before reading the charts.

Note: If possible, obtain recordings of compositions using the rondo form. Your music specialist may be able to assist you. Many of the last movements of symphonies by classical composers are written in the rondo form. Some of the more modern composers have used the rondo form with interesting harmonies. The older children might find these recordings quite exciting:

Troika, Lieutenant Kije' Suite, and *Opus 60* by S. Prokofiev, *Swingin' Round* and *The Riddle* by the Dave Brubeck Quartet

EVALUATION OF RHYTHMIC AND PERCEPTUAL SKILLS

Aural Acuity and Perception

1. Can the children hear an established rhythm pattern and create a variation of the pattern without losing the beat?
2. Can they create melodies to original rhythm patterns and perform them as part of the rondo?
3. Can they listen to a rondo on a recording and identify the form by using A B A C etc.?

Visual Acuity and Perception

1. Are the children becoming increasingly confident with more complex rhythm patterns?
2. Can they read the patterns on the chart unassisted without losing the beat?

Sixteenth Notes

The quarter note (♩) has no bar; the eighth note (♫) has one bar; the sixteenth note (♬♬) has two bars. Refer to Lesson 4.

If any of the children in the class are taking instrumental instruction on a wind instrument (trumpet, clarinet, flute, etc.) ask them to demonstrate the technique of "tongueing" on their respective instruments.

Note: This technique will vary with the instrument and the instructor from "too–doo –too–doo" to "tak–a–tak–a," but the children will relate the tongueing syllables to the rhythm syllables used for the sixteenth notes. While reading these rhythmic exercises containing sixteenth notes, accent the first sixteenth note to make the reading easier (ti–di–ti–di)

INTRODUCE THE CHART

1. Ask the class to read the words and clap the pattern of the first two lines on the chart.
2. Ask the class to create words to the last line of the chart. Accept any words that are rhythmically and syllabically correct. Some examples might be:

> coal mines, coal mines, West Vir-gin-ia coal mines • sand-wich, sand-wich, pea-nut but-ter sand-wich

Note: The reason for asking the children to create their own verbal combinations to a rhythm pattern is so that they will be more aware of various rhythm symbols through syllabication.

3. Read and clap the entire chart with rhythm syllables.
4. Step the beat, read, and clap the chart with rhythm syllables or words.

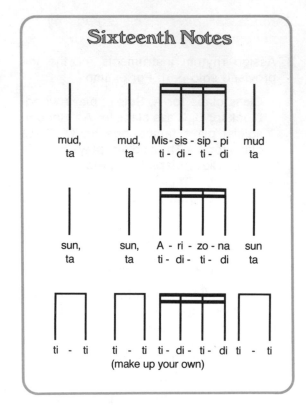

Sixteenth Notes

mud, / ta   mud, / ta   Mis-sis-sip-pi / ti-di-ti-di   mud / ta

sun, / ta   sun, / ta   A-ri-zo-na / ti-di-ti-di   sun / ta

ti - ti   ti - ti   ti-di-ti-di   ti - ti
(make up your own)

5. While seated at their desks, have the children tap the beat with their left hands and tap the rhythm pattern on the chart with their right hands.
6. Sing a familiar song in duple time (e.g., "Yankee Doodle," "This Train," "Are You Sleeping?"). While singing the song, step the beat and clap or tap one line of the chart, repeating it as many times as necessary to complete the song. Keep the beat on the chart while the children are singing.
7. Turn to the next lesson.

Note: The next five charts all deal with sixteenth notes, and therefore the "Evaluation" for these charts is given at the end of Lesson 34.

PREPARATION FOR THE CHART

Note: Although many of the songs the children have sung contained sixteenth notes, this will be the first time they will read the rhythmic notation. You may wish to point out that whenever a bar is added to a group of notes the duration becomes twice as fast.

Can You Read?

eraser end of the pencil for tonal differentiation.

3. Sing a familiar song. Step the beat and clap one of the rhythm patterns on the chart while singing.

Note: For the more musically capable children, try clapping the entire chart while singing the song.

4. Divide the class into two or more groups and clap the chart as a canon, repeating the chart several times without losing the beat. Use a different tone quality for each group. For example,

    Group 1—tap with pencils
    Group 2—rap knuckles on desk
    Group 3—clap, softly
    Group 4—pat knees

5. Divide the class into four groups and sing the chart as a round. Sing "do" for the first line, "mi" for the second line, "sol" for the third line, "high do" for the fourth line. Repeat the chart several times.

6. Read and clap Charts 30 and 31 with rhythm syllables.

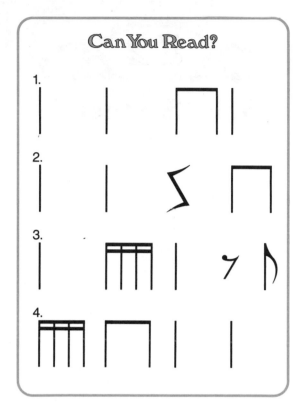

INTRODUCE THE CHART

1. Read and clap the rhythm pattern with rhythm syllables while stepping the beat. Keep a moderately slow tempo and move from line to line without losing the beat.

2. Tap the beat with the left hand and tap the pattern with the right hand, using the

ADDITIONAL ACTIVITIES

1. *Dictation by Teacher or Leader.* This activity may be written or used with individual rhythm charts.

Teacher claps	Class echoes with syllables and writes
	ta triple-ti ta ta
	ta ti di ti di ta rest

2. *Flash Cards.* Give each child an opportunity to clap a pattern using sixteenth notes with rhythm syllables.

3. Turn to the next lesson.

More Sixteenth Notes

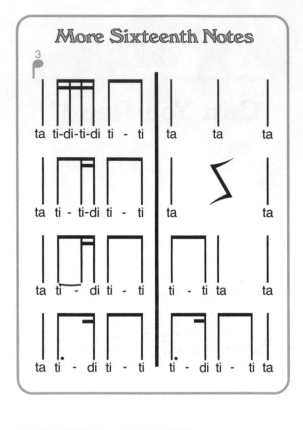

INTRODUCE THE CHART

1. Ask the class how many beats there are to a measure on this chart. (3)
2. What happens to the tied note? (silent but given and held for its full value)
3. Review the dotted note. (Chart 12)

   Note: The dot gets half the value of the note it comes after. Draw attention to the similarity between the dotted note and the tie:

   ♩. = ♩♩   ♩. = ♩♩   ♪. = ♪♪

4. Step the beat and clap the pattern on the chart with rhythm syllables, stepping in 3/4 time (step tip-toe).
5. Tap the beat (meter) on the desk with the left hand, accent the first beat, and tap the pattern on the chart with the right hand using rhythm syllables.
6. Divide the class into two groups. Have Group 1 read and clap the first measure and Group 2 read and clap the second measure, both groups using rhythm syllables.
7. Divide the class into two or more groups and clap the chart as a round.
8. Divide the class into two groups and have them sing the chart by following your hand signals, using a different syllable for each measure. Use two hand singing: left hand signals for Group 1 and right hand signals for Group 2. Begin this activity by using one syllable for each measure.

ADDITIONAL ACTIVITIES

1. *Dictation:* Dictate various rhythm patterns using the dotted eighth and sixteenth notes. This activity can be done in either duple or triple meter (♪♩).

Teacher claps	Class echoes with syllables and writes

   ta ti di ti di ti di ta

   ti ta ti ti di ta

2. *Echo Clapping.* Choose several children to lead the class in echo clapping, using syncopation and sixteenth notes.
3. Turn to the next lesson.

Mystery Songs

Mystery Songs

KOOKABURRA

Australian Round

Kook-a-bur-ra sits in the old gum tree;

Mer-ry, mer-ry king of the bush is he.___

Laugh, kook-a-bur-ra, laugh, kook-a-bur-ra,

Gay your life must be.

PREPARATION FOR THE CHART

1. Teach the songs and use previous rhythmic and melodic experiences.
2. Sing the songs and clap the pattern, step the beat, where possible, turn the phrases.
3. Ask individual children to conduct the class while they sing the song.

   Note: Before introducing the chart, be sure the class is familiar with the songs.

4. Ask individual children to clap the pattern of one of the songs as a mystery song for the class to identify.

INTRODUCE THE CHART

1. Clap one of the patterns on the chart for the class to identify. The child who correctly identifies the pattern may clap the pattern with rhythm syllables.
   - Can anyone in the class identify the song?
   - The child who correctly identifies the song may conduct the class while they sing.
2. Continue through the entire chart by clapping the pattern, identifying the pattern, clapping the pattern with rhythm syllables, identifying the song, and sing-

STAR SPANGLED BANNER
Words by Francis Scott Key

Oh, say, can you see by the dawn's ear - ly light,

What so proud - ly we hailed at the twi - light's last gleam - ing?

Whose broad stripes and bright stars, through the per - il - ous fight,

O'er the ram - parts we watched were so gal - lant - ly stream - ing.

And the rock - ets' red glare, the bombs burst - ing in air,

Gave proof through the night that our flag was still there.

Oh, say, does that star - spang - led ban - ner yet wave

O'er the land of the free and the home of the brave?

ing the song while using various rhythmic activities.

OTHER SONGS TO USE

Clap the rhythm pattern of a familiar song or put a fragment of the identifying pattern on the chalkboard. Some songs are:

- "Cherries So Ripe"

- "Riding in a Buggy"

- "Sweetly Sings the Donkey"

Choose different children to clap these patterns for the class to identify.

ADDITIONAL ACTIVITIES

1. *Dictation:* Patterns may be written on paper or individual rhythm charts:

Teacher claps | Class echoes with rhythm syllables and writes

ti di ti di ti ti di ti ti ti ti

Clap as many pattern variations as you feel your class can do successfully.

2. Using the patterns the children have written, tap the beat with the left hand and the pattern with the right hand. Tell the

70

I SAW A RABBIT

Kentucky Folk Song

Solo Rab-bit run all a-round the town! **Chorus** How do you know? **Solo** Saw him chased by a big black hound!

Chorus Who told you so? **Solo** I saw a rab-bit, uh-huh! **Chorus** **Solo** I saw a rab-bit, uh-huh! **Chorus**

Solo I saw a rab-bit, uh-huh! **Chorus** **Solo** I caught a rab-bit, oh! **Chorus**

---

children to mark the patterns they have written with measure bars.

Note: You may have to tell the class the number of beats in a measure when this activity is introduced but later they will be *able to feel the pulse and mark the measures without assistance.*

3. Turn to the next lesson.

The Old Brass Wagon

The Old Brass Wagon

Cir-cle to the left, the Old Brass Wa-gon;

Cir-cle to the left, the Old Brass Wa-gon;

Cir-cle to the left, the Old Brass Wa-gon;

You're the one my dar-ling.

PREPARATION FOR THE CHART

1. Teach the song. There are many verses to this familiar song which can be found in music texts and folk song collections. Teach as many verses as you feel your children will enjoy.
2. Sing the song and use previous rhythmic experiences. Clap, step, or walk the beat; turn the phrase, use inner hearing flash cards.

INTRODUCE THE CHART

1. Ask for volunteers to read and clap the rhythm pattern on the chart with rhythm syllables.

2. Point to various notes on the chart and ask individual children to name the tone syllable with the correct hand signal.
3. *Read* the chart slowly with tone syllables and hand signals, but *do not sing*. Do the children have the correct spatial relationship of the intervals?

    Line 1: ddddd d d d d l, s,
    Line 2: rrrrr r s, s, l, d
    Line 3: mmmmm m m r d l, d
    Line 4: r m s, l, d d

Note: It may be necessary to review low la (l,) and low sol (s,) in Chart 11.

4. Sing the chart slowly with tone syllables

and hand signals. To reinforce the spatial relationship of the intervals, refer to Chart 9 (vertical scale):

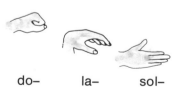

do–   la–   sol–

Establish the pitch for the starting note before beginning to sing.

5. Sing the chart with words and hand signals. The children will enjoy increasing the tempo for each verse.

ADDITIONAL ACTIVITIES

1. *Melodic Dictation:* Sing or play various melodic patterns for the class to write on staff paper or individual charts. Establish the position of the starting note (i.e., "sol is on the third space.")

Teacher sings or plays	Class echoes with syllables and writes
begin on 3rd space "sol"	

s mmmm r d

begin on 1st line "do"

d r m s l l l d'

Note: Use rhythm patterns and melodies that are within the musical competencies of the class. Make the melodies and rhythmic patterns simple enough to ensure success, but difficult enough to be challenging.

2. Divide the class into two groups. Have one group sing and step the pattern of the first measure of Lines 1, 2, and 3 of the chart, while the second group sings and claps the last measure ("Old Brass Wagon"); both groups sing, clap, and step the last line.

3. Create an instrumental accompaniment for the song. For example,

woodblock: ⊓ ⊓
tambourine: ⊓⊓⊓ ⊓

EVALUATION OF RHYTHMIC AND PERCEPTUAL SKILLS

Psychomotor Development and Perception

1. Can the children use hand signals with confidence and increasing motor control?
2. Can they approach a new concept with ease and confidence?

Aural Acuity and Perception

1. Can the children hear rhythm patterns with dotted eighth notes (⌐⌐) and sixteenth notes (⊓⊓⊓)?
2. Can they hear tonal patterns using dotted eighths, sixteenth notes, and low (la (l,) and low sol (s,)?
3. Can they write these patterns on the staff?

Visual Acuity and Perception

1. Can the children conceptualize the position of the tonal patterns as seen on a chart with hand signals?
2. Can they read a familiar song written on the staff with rhythm syllables or tone syllables?

A New Note-Fa

A New Note – Fa

sol

Mystery Song

sol 4
do

sol
do

Fa

CHAIRS TO MEND

Traditional Round

1
sol
Chairs to mend, old chairs to mend?

2
Mack - er - el, fresh mack - er - el.

3
An - y old rags, an - y old rags?

The next four charts all teach the same basic concept, and therefore the "Evaluation" for these charts appears at the end of Lesson 38.

PREPARATION FOR THE CHART

1. Teach the song.
2. Sing the song and clap the beat.
3. Sing the song, step the beat, clap the pattern, and turn the phrase.
4. Divide the class into 3 groups and sing as a round.

Note: Many folk songs use "fa" as a passing tone although it is not a part of the common pentatonic scale. In western music, the syllable "ti" is often used as a leading tone to "do" and can be taught by rote. The "ti" will be introduced on a later chart. The hand signal for "ti" is the forefinger pointed upward toward "do."

INTRODUCE THE CHART

1. Establish the relationship of fa to sol and mi by using the five fingers to demonstrate the five lines of the staff.
   - If sol is here   where is fa?

   - If mi is here   where is fa?

   - Vary the position of sol and mi on the hand and ask individual children to find fa.
   - For the more musical children, find fa by starting on various notes of the scale.

     If do is here   where is fa?

     If re is here   where is fa?

2. Sing several melodic patterns with hand signals for the children to echo:

Teacher sings	Class echoes with hand signals
⊓ | ⊓ | d r m m f s	⊓ | ⊓ | d r m m f s
⊓ ⊓ ⊓ | s f m f s s s	⊓ ⊓ ⊓ | s f m f s s s

Make these patterns as difficult as you feel your class can handle successfully.

3. Ask several children to sing the first line of the chart with hand signals. Allow each child to establish his own pitch for sol, and have the class echo with hand signals.
4. Choose one child to clap the pattern of the mystery song with rhythm syllables. Did the class recognize the song?
5. Sing the two phrases on the chart with hand signals and tone syllables with the class. Begin the song at a moderately slow tempo to give the class confidence while moving from syllable to syllable.
6. Sing the first two phrases of the song with tone syllables and hand signals and complete the song with words. (Many of the children will be able to sing the last phrase with tone syllables and hand signals.)

   ⊓ ♩ | ⊓ ♩ |
   s, s, d   d   s, s, d   d
   An-y old rags, an-y old rags?

7. Tell the class the interval from sol to fa is a **major** second and the interval from fa to mi is a **minor** second.

Note: A piano keyboard or full set of resonator bells will enable the children to visualize this concept.

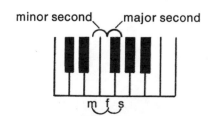

minor second   major second

m f s

OTHER SONGS TO USE

"Come, Let's Sing" (Chart 12)

³ ♩ | ♩ | ⊓ | | ♩ |
s f m r d t, d r m f

"Hymn to Joy"—Symphony No. 9 by Beethoven (last movement)

⁴ | | | | | | | | | | | | | | |. ♪ | ♩
m m f s s f m r d d r m m r r

"Three Blind Mice"

⁶ |. |. |. ♩. |. |. |. ♩. |. | ♪ |. ♩. | ♪ |. ♩.
m r d   m r d   s f f m   s f f m

ADDITIONAL ACTIVITIES

1. Divide the class into two or three groups and sing the song as a round, using tone syllables or words. Use hand signals for the entire song.
2. Create a rhythmic ostinato for instruments while the class sings the round. For example,

   woodblock ⊓ ♩ | ⊓ ♩ |
   drum |. ♪ | | |. ♪ | |

3. Make flash cards of various melodic patterns using fa. Each child should have an opportunity to sing one of the melodic patterns with tone syllables and hand signals:

| | ⊓ | s l s f m	⊓ ⊓ ⊓ | d r m f s s s	⊓ | ⊓ | m f s s f m

4. Establish the pitch for sol. Make hand signals of various patterns using fa but *do not* sing. Have the class sing the pattern with hand signals. Later, ask individ-

ual children to lead the class or sing the patterns.

Teacher or leader   Class

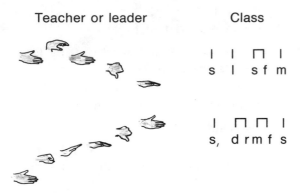

```
I   I   ⊓   I
s   l   s f  m
```

```
I   ⊓  ⊓   I
s,  d r m f  s
```

5. *Intervals:* This activity was first introduced in Level 1, and should be used with those children who are musically capable. The use of the Vertical Scale (Chart 9) will provide a visual approach to the recognition of the intervals being sung. Begin the activity with familiar intervals:

Teacher sings syllables with hand signals	Class sings intervals
⊓ I ⊓ I ⊓ I ⊓ I	
s s m s s m mi-nor third mi-nor third	
⊓ ⊓ ⊓ ⊓ ⊓ ⊓ ⊓ ⊓	
s s f f s s f f ma-jor sec-ond ma-jor sec-ond	

Continue with intervals previously introduced.

6. Turn to the next lesson.

Michael, Row the Boat Ashore

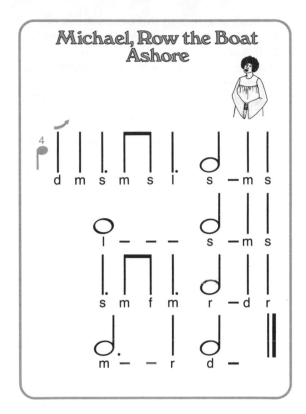

PREPARATION FOR THE CHART

Note: There are many verses to this song which can be found in music texts. Encourage the children to make up their own verses and sing the solo part, with the class singing the response, "Hallelujah!"

1. Teach the song and sing as many verses as you feel your class will enjoy. Encourage individual children to sing the solo part.
2. Sing the song and step the beat **alla breve** (2 steps to the measure).
3. Sing the song and use previous rhythmic experiences.

Note: The rhythm pattern of this song will provide a real challenge to most classes.

Stepping the beat and clapping the pattern will enable many of the children to give each note its full value and simplify the syncopation.

INTRODUCE THE CHART

1. Read and clap the rhythm pattern with rhythm syllables. This chart represents a combination of many rhythmic experiences: syncopation, dotted notes, half-notes whole notes, and anacrusis. Establish the beat by saying "One, two, ta, ta," using a fairly slow tempo so that each note will receive full value.
2. Read and clap the rhythm pattern and step the beat (4).
3. Speak the tone syllables with hand sig-

nals while keeping the beat on the chart.

4. Sing the entire chart with tone syllables and hand signals.
5. Sing the entire chart with words and hand signals.
6. Choose one child to lead the class with hand signals while they sing the song.

Note: Encourage as many children as possible to lead the class in hand singing. This will prove to be invaluable in developing ear training and aural accuracy.

ADDITIONAL ACTIVITIES

1. Sing the song, turn the phrase, and clap the pattern. (This is a highly integrated activity.)
2. Tap the beat in four (4) with the left hand and tap the pattern with the right hand, while singing the song.
3. Sing the song by phrases. Establish the position for "do" on the musical staff, and write the melody on staff paper, individual charts, or the chalkboard.

Note: "Do" should be placed on the staff to avoid the use of ledger lines at the beginning of this activity:

Ask the children to put in the measure lines. Did they remember the anacrusis?

4. Turn to the next lesson.

A New Note-Ti

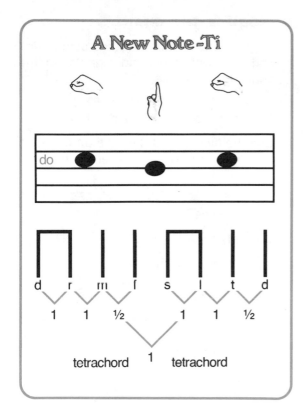

A New Note-Ti

do

| d | r | m | f | s | l | t | d |

1   1   ½   1   1   ½

tetrachord   1   tetrachord

Ti

Note: The presentation of ti will serve to introduce the complete diatonic scale which is the melodic basis for much of our western music. The interval of the natural minor second or half-steps in the major diatonic scale (mi–fa and ti–do) is sometimes difficult for children to hear and sing correctly if there has not been sufficient background in the singing of syllables.

PREPARATION FOR THE CHART

1. Review one of the following songs
   • "Au Clair de la Lune" (Chart 5), "Come, Let's Sing" (Chart 13), "Mr. Banjo" (Chart 16), or "Kookaburra" (Chart 33).

2. Sing the song and use previous rhythmic and melodic experiences.
3. Turn to the Vertical Scale (Chart 9) and sing one of the songs with hand signals on the chart. Make the hand signals on the chart and move slowly from syllable to syllable while singing. For example, using "Come Let's Sing":

$$\frac{3}{4}$$ ♩ l | ♩ l | ⌐ l l | ♩ l etc.
s – f | m – r | d t, d r | m – f

Let the children discover the new note. Tell them the new syllable is called "ti" and the hand signal is made by pointing up to "do."

INTRODUCE THE CHART

1. Sing several rhythm patterns using "do" and "ti" with the hand signals on the chart. For example,

2. Use the five fingers to find ti on the staff.
   - If "do" is here   where is ti?

   - If la is here   where is ti?

   - Begin with "do" and then progress to other syllables of the diatonic scales, depending on the musical abilities of the class.

3. Put a five line staff on the chalkboard, or have the children use individual staff charts. Place various notes on the staff. For example, Sol is on the second line, where is ti? Mi is on the second space, where is ti? Re is on the first space, where is ti?

4. Clap the rhythm pattern on the chart. Sing the complete ascending scale, using hand signals. Follow the rhythm pattern on the chart.

5. Ask individual children to sing the complete ascending scale with hand signals, observing the spatial relationship of the intervals. Let each child establish his own starting pitch.

   Note: The numbers and fractions at the bottom of the chart give the construction of a major diatonic scale with whole steps and half-steps. The following activity will prove exciting to children with musical talent. With this formula the children will be able to construct a major scale on any note.

6. Show the class a full set of resonator bells or a piano keyboard:

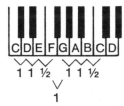

   Ask one child to find two white notes that are next to one another and not separated by a black note (E–F or B–C). Tell the children these are natural half-steps (minor seconds). All the other white notes have a black note between them and are called whole steps (major seconds).

7. Start on C and play and sing with syllables the first four white notes. This is the **lower tetrachord** of the C major scale.

8. Start on G and play and sing the next four white notes with syllables (starting with sol). This is the **upper tetrachord** of the C major scale.

   Note: Tell the class there is always a whole step between each tetrachord. Add this word to their musical vocabulary. Ask the children to look in the dictionary for the meaning of the prefix "tetra." There are some exciting words using this prefix.

ADDITIONAL ACTIVITIES

Note: These last activities may seem difficult and technical to the nonmusician, but many children at this level are beginning to show musical talent or may be playing a musical instrument. The following activities will be merely an exposure to the construction of a diatonic scale and will enable the children to explore and experiment in a meaningful experience. The use of the formula for the tetrachord will make it possible to build a major scale on any tone they choose.

1. Ask one child to find G on the piano or resonator bells. (Some children will need assistance.) Can he play a major scale starting on G, using the formula for the tetrachord? What happens when he plays

ti or the seventh of the scale? How can he follow the formula? (Raising the F to F♯)

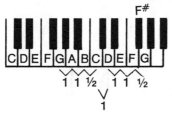

F#

C D E F G A B C D E F G

1 1 ½   1 1 ½

V
1

Build a major scale on F. If the formula is followed, the B must be lowered to B♭. Remember, the letter names of the notes must be in consecutive order (A B C D E F G A, etc.).

*Note: The **sharp** (♯) raises the note a half-step, and the **flat** (♭) lowers the note a half-step.*

2. Turn to the next lesson.

All Through the Night

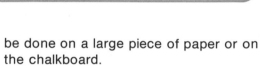

PREPARATION FOR THE CHART

1. Teach the song. Use previous rhythmic and melodic experiences.
2. Ask the children what dynamics should be used with this song. Should the song be loud (*f*) or soft and tender (*p*)?

Note: Be sure the class is thoroughly familiar with the song before introducing the chart.

INTRODUCE THE CHART

1. Read and clap the rhythm pattern on the chart with rhythm syllables. If the children are insecure, step the beat while clapping the pattern. Choose several children to read and clap the chart for the class.

2. Read and sing the chart with hand signals and tone syllables. Observe the class and note the spatial relationship of the intervals while they are using hand signals. The correct use of hand singing will enable the children to realize and hear tonal relationships, both visually and aurally.
3. Read and sing the chart with hand signals and words while stepping the beat. Ask individual children to read the chart and sing the song with hand signals.

ADDITIONAL ACTIVITIES

1. *Melodic Contour and Form.* With large arm movements, make a picture of the melody in the air. This activity can also be done on a large piece of paper or on the chalkboard.
   - Can the children discover the similarities and differences within the melody?
   - How many times is the first phrase repeated? (3)
   - What is the form of the song? (A A B A)

2. *Inner Hearing.* Using hand signals, sing the first word of the song ("Sleep"), and use inner hearing until "All Through the Night."
   - Did all the children enter on the correct beat and tone?

ALL THROUGH THE NIGHT

Welsh Folk Song

A. Sleep, my child, and peace at-tend thee,
A. Guard-ian an-gels God will send thee,

All through the night.
All through the night.

B. Soft the drow-sy hours are creep-ing,

Hill and vale in slum-ber steep-ing,

A. I my lov-ing vi-gil keep-ing,

All through the night.

Visual Acuity and Perception

1. Can the children visualize the spatial relationships of various intervals using ti and fa?
2. Can they find ti and fa on the musical staff when given another syllable of the diatonic scale?

Musical Development and Social Maturity

1. Can the children construct a major diatonic scale on the piano or resonator bells, using the formula for the tetrachord?
2. Do they express a desire to explore and discover other major diatonic scales on the piano or resonator bells?

• Continue this activity through the entire song.

EVALUATION OF RHYTHMIC AND PERCEPTUAL SKILLS

Aural Acuity and Perception

1. Can the children hear the interval of the minor second (mi–fa and ti–do) in a major diatonic scale and in a familiar song?
2. Can they hear and recognize similarities and differences in a familiar song?

Echo Round

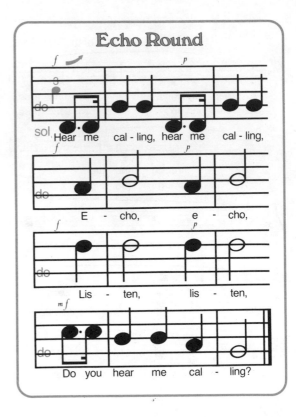

Note: Charts 39 and 40 provide a culmination of the Level Two experiences, and therefore the "Evaluation" for these charts is given at the end of Lesson 40.

PREPARATION FOR THE CHART

When the musical notation is on the chart, the class can learn the song by using previous rhythmic and melodic experiences.
- Determine the beat.
- Read and clap the rhythm pattern.
- Discover the anacrusis.
- Sing the intervals with tone syllables.
- Observe the dynamic markings.

INTRODUCE THE CHART

1. Read and clap the rhythm pattern on the chart with rhythm syllables. Establish the beat by saying, "One, two, ti–di ta ta, etc." Use a fairly slow tempo.
2. Read and clap the rhythm pattern with rhythm syllables and step the beat.
3. Choose one child to read and clap the first three beats of Line 1 with rhythm syllables. Have the class echo:

Leader	Class
⊓			⊓		
ti–di ta ta	ti–di ta ta

Continue clapping and echoing through the entire chart. Clap the last line of the chart (4) in its entirety before the class echoes.

4. Sing the first three beats of Line 1 with tone syllables and hand signals. Have the class echo with hand signals:

Teacher	Class
⊓			⊓		
s, s, d d	s, s, d d

Continue through Lines 2 and 3. Sing all of Line 4 for the class to echo:

5. Select one child to lead the class in the last activity.

Teacher	Class
⌐┐ | | | ♩	⌐┐ | | | ♩
f f m m r d	f f m m r d

6. Sing the entire chart with tone syllables and hand signals, observing the dynamic markings.
7. Sing the entire chart with words and hand signals.

ADDITIONAL ACTIVITIES

Note: This song is invaluable for encouraging the shy or nonparticipating child to become a part of the group.

1. Have the class sing the first three beats of the song ("Hear me calling?") Point to one child to be the echo. It is most important that the beat be constant. If one child does not respond, keep the beat going and continue the song. Repeat the song several times in order to give several children an opportunity to be the echo.
2. Use inner hearing flash cards. Perform a different activity for each line of the song:

   Line 1: step
   Line 2: clap
   Line 3: feel
   Line 4: sing

3. Sing the song as a two, three, or four part round, depending on the musical ability of the class.
4. Divide the class into two, three, or four groups and step the pattern of the song as a round.
5. Choose one child to lead the class in two-hand singing. Divide the class into two groups. Use hand signals with the right hand for Group 1, and hand signals with the left hand for Group 2. Have the entire class use arm signals for Line 4.
6. Turn to the next lesson.

Frog Music

Frog Music

1.
1. There once was a frog who jumped in a bog
2. His music was short, for soon he was caught,

2.
and played the bass fid - dle in the
and now in the mid - dle of a

Frog Music
continued

3.
mid - dle of a pud-dle what a mud-dle!
grid - dle he is fry - ing and is cry - ing!

4.
" Bet - ter go round! Bet - ter go round! "
" Rath-er be drowned! Rath-er be drowned! "

PREPARATION FOR THE CHART

Note: This song utilizes many previous learning experiences, both rhythmic and melodic.

1. Echo clap, using combinations of:
   - Eighth notes: ti–ti.
   - Sixteenth notes: ti–di–ti–di
   - Triplets: trip–le–ti
   - Half-notes: ta–a
   - Tied half-notes: ta–a–a
   - Whole notes: ta–a–a–a
   - Rests: ▬ ▬ ⸲ ⸲

2. Use canon clapping with these rhythms in various combinations. Encourage individuals to lead the class in echo and canon clapping.

3. Echo sing with tone syllables, using low sol (s,) and low la (l,) with hand signals:

Teacher or leader	Class echoes
l ⌐ l l	l ⌐ l l
d l, l, s, d	d l, l, s, d
⌐ l ⌐ l	⌐ l ⌐ l
d r m m f s	d r m m f s

4. Use two-hand singing with the syllables previously learned. For example,

R.H. s - l - s - f - m - r - d
L.H. s m - r - d - l, - s, - d -

INTRODUCE THE CHART

Note: Encourage the children to read a new rhythm pattern with little or no assis-tance. Be sure to keep the beat as you move back and forth between charts.

1. Read and clap the rhythm pattern of the song with rhythm syllables while stepping the beat.
   - Begin by stepping the beat to prepare for the anacrusis.

   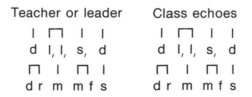
   step step ti | ti ti–di ti–ti etc.

   - Observe the repeat bars and be sure to give the triplet its full value.

2. Read the words, clap the pattern, and step the beat.

3. Read the intervals on the chart silently and with hand signals, using inner hear-ing.

Note: Observe the class for spatial relationship of the intervals. Let the children discover that the melody consists of five tones (s, d r m f s) that proceed in a stepwise pattern except for the anacrusis (s,).

4. Establish the pitch for s, and sing the chart with hand signals and tone syllables, using a fairly slow tempo.

Note: This activity will pose very few problems for the class that has had sufficient melodic and rhythmic experiences.

5. Sing the chart with words and hand signals, observing the repeat bars.
6. Divide the class into two or three groups and sing the song as a round.

ADDITIONAL ACTIVITIES

1. Divide the class into three groups and clap the rhythm pattern as a round.
   - This activity can also be played on rhythm instruments of varying tone qualities.
   - For a more vigorous activity, try stepping the pattern as a two or three part round while singing the song.

2. For a truly exciting musical experience, close the chart and ask the class to use inner hearing and write the rhythm pattern of "Frog Music" on individual charts or staff paper. Remember to put in the measure bars.
3. Ask three musically capable children to sing the song as a round for the class.

EVALUATION AND SUMMARY

Psychomotor Development and Perception

Can the children perform integrated rhythmic activities with confidence? That is,
- singing and stepping or walking the beat.
- singing and turning the phrase.
- clapping the pattern and stepping or walking the beat.
- clapping the beat and stepping the pattern while singing the song.
- singing and tapping or playing an ostinato.
- singing and stepping or walking a canon or round.
- canon clapping.

Aural Acuity and Perception

1. Can the children hear and recognize the various intervals of the major diatonic and pentatonic scales?
2. Can they sing and name the interval sung? That is,
   - sol–mi—minor third
   - sol–la—major second
   - la–mi—perfect fourth
   - mi–do—major third
   - re–do—major second
   - sol–do—perfect fifth
   - mi–fa—minor second
   - ti,–do—minor second
   - do–do'—octave
3. Can they hear and recognize various rhythm patterns containing syncopation, sixteenth notes, and rests?

Visual Acuity and Perception

1. Can the children read and perform various rhythm patterns using combinations of note values?
2. Can they read the tone syllables on the chart with ease?

Musical Development and Social Maturity

1. Do the children participate and contribute with enthusiasm, involvement, and confidence?
2. Can they identify similarities and differences and recognize simple forms in music? For example,

   A B A, Rondo, etc.

3. Can they use musical terms with growing confidence and follow musical directions such as beat • phrase • anacrusis • ostinato • piano • forte • etc.?
4. Do they exercise musical discrimination in the use of instruments • dynamics • tone quality • etc.?
5. Do the children derive personal satisfaction from their musical achievement?

Hand Signals

Do

Re

Mi

Fa

Sol

La

Ti

Do'

88